BLITZ KIDS

Also by Duncan Barrett & Nuala Calvi

The Sugar Girls

The Sugar Girls of Love Lane

GI Brides

The Girls Who Went to War

By Duncan Barrett

Hitler's British Isles

Men of Letters

Duncan Barrett and Nuala Calvi

BLITZ KIDS

True Stories from the Children of Wartime Britain

H

HEADLINE

First published in 2025 by Headline Publishing Group Limited

1

Cataloguing in Publication Data is available from the British Library.

Paperback ISBN: 978 1 4722 8597 3

Typeset by EM&EN
Printed and bound in Great Britain by Clays Ltd, Elcograf S.p.A.

Headline's policy is to use papers that are natural, renewable and recyclable
products and made from wood grown in well-managed forests and other
controlled sources. The logging and manufacturing processes are expected
to conform to the environmental regulations of the country of origin.

MIX
Paper | Supporting
responsible forestry
FSC® C104740
FSC
www.fsc.org

Headline Publishing Group Limited
An Hachette UK Company
Carmelite House
50 Victoria Embankment
London EC4Y 0DZ

The authorized representative in the EEA is Hachette Ireland,
8 Castlecourt Centre, Dublin 15, D15 XTP3, Ireland (email: info@hbgi.ie)

www.headline.co.uk
www.hachette.co.uk

For Leo

Contents

Preface

A hard, jagged lump of metal has been sitting on the bookshelf in our study for over a decade. It's a piece of shrapnel from the Second World War – an ugly, spiky little thing that can nick your finger if you're not careful. But to a young lad called Henry, who discovered it in 1940, still warm from an air raid during the London Blitz, it was a piece of treasure.

Henry gave us this little chunk of history back in 2011, while we were researching our first book, *The Sugar Girls*. We had come to hear stories about the Tate & Lyle factories in East London, but as so often happens during our interviews, reminiscing about the past took Henry all the way back to his childhood. Soon he was telling us about growing up in the East End amidst air-raid sirens and falling bombs, and as he handed us the unremarkable scrap of metal and described the excitement he had felt at finding it in the rubble, his eyes lit up like a little boy again.

A year or so ago, when we were looking for our next project, Henry's piece of shrapnel caught our eye. We remembered his story, and decided we wanted to find out more about all the children who had lived through such an extraordinary time. It also reminded us that it was when people talked about their childhoods that they smiled the most, talked the most, remembered the most – even though those memories went back the furthest. Having written several books about grown-ups' experiences during the war, we wanted to tell the story through the eyes of children.

With the eightieth anniversary of VE Day approaching in May 2025, the project felt even more pressing. For most 'Blitz Kids', this will be the last major anniversary they live to see. Their generation is rapidly passing, and we knew this was our last chance to capture their stories.

Children are often forgotten at moments of commemoration, when the achievements and sacrifices of adults take centre stage. Yet there were more than 10 million children living in this country at the start of the war, and they form an important part of the history of homefront Britain.

It was something the king himself recognised at the time. One of our interviewees proudly showed us a letter George VI had sent to every schoolchild in Britain in 1946, thanking them for the role they had played in the war effort:

> To-day, as we celebrate victory, I send this personal message to you and all other boys and girls at school. For you have shared in the hardships and dangers of a total war and you have shared no less in the triumph of the Allied Nations.

I know you will always feel proud to belong to a country which was capable of such supreme effort; proud too, of parents and elder brothers and sisters who by their courage, endurance and enterprise brought victory. May these qualities be yours as you grow up and join in the common effort to establish among the nations of the world unity and peace.

For decades, the abiding image of children during the Second World War has been a little boy or girl with a name tag around their neck, carrying their gas mask in a cardboard box as they step on to a steam train that will take them away to safety in the countryside. But the evacuee experience is only part of the wartime story. While we were keen to speak to former evacuees as well, we particularly wanted to know what had happened to those who stayed behind. The children who didn't go away – or didn't stay away – and instead lived through the Blitz alongside their parents and older siblings.

What was it like for these children who experienced the Blitz close-up, who spent their nights in cold, cramped air-raid shelters with the rumble of planes and the crash of bombs overhead? How did their young minds make sense of what was going on around them? And what on earth could their parents say to reassure them, when up above someone really was trying to kill them? During the war, 7,736 British children lost their lives thanks to enemy action, accounting for one in eight civilian deaths. Thousands more were injured, many of them seriously.

We now know that the first few years of a child's life are crucial to building a sense of security in the world and learning to form healthy attachments. What happens to a generation whose first few years of life are among the most dangerous in history? A generation whose early attachments may be severed – not just by evacuation but by fathers being called up to fight, and parents, grandparents, uncles and aunts being wiped out by German bombs?

As parents ourselves, we had seen the impact on children of a more recent global crisis – the Covid-19 pandemic. We witnessed first-hand the repercussions for children's mental health, not to mention the disruption to their education. But at least now we have the language to talk about what they've been through, and the psychological interventions to address it. Neither of those things existed in 1940s Britain. Children who experienced the horrors of the Blitz were generally left to 'just get on with it'.

How did the inevitable trauma this generation carried affect them, both at the time and later in life? And how did their young minds, subject to the double censorship of the government and their parents, who did their best to hide uncomfortable truths about the war, make sense of the madness going on in the world around them?

We wanted to find out.

Tracking down people in their late eighties and nineties isn't easy. They're often living in care homes or sheltered accommodation, where staff are rightly suspicious of strangers who knock on the door asking to speak to the residents. They're not usually in Facebook groups or on local history forums and don't often make it out to bingo nights, coffee mornings or community centres, although we did find people in all those places too.

In some cases, interviewees' children saw posts we had put on social media and got in touch, although they understandably wanted reassurance that we were who we said we were. 'How do I know you're not con artists?' one man asked before he would let us meet his elderly mother.

Some relatives insisted on sitting in on our interviews, and often proved incredibly helpful at jogging their parents' memories or repeating our questions at a louder volume. Sometimes they ended up learning things they'd never known about their own family history. One woman's grown-up daughters were shocked to discover that the patch of grass they'd played on as children was the spot where their mother's best friend Pamela had lived, until a bomb fell on the house and killed her. 'I'll never forget you, Pamela,' their mother kept repeating, her eyes filled with tears.

Our research for this book took us all over the country. We were keen to focus not just on the Blitz in London – famous throughout the world – but on the less well-known blitzes in other British cities as well. Given the time constraints, we weren't able to cover all of them, but we aimed for as wide a geographical spread as possible, including Birmingham, Liverpool, Coventry, Southampton, Bristol and Belfast.

As a result, our research involved a lot of travel to unfamiliar places, and getting to grips with the geography not just of the present but of the past. We spent many hours wandering around in search of streets that didn't exist any more, and discovering parks and housing estates on the site of bombed-out houses, schools, churches or factories. We wondered if the people living in these communities now had any idea of the tragic events that had taken place there all those years earlier.

One positive legacy of the Covid-19 pandemic is that many elderly people are now comfortable using Zoom, and as a result we were able to cast our net as widely as possible, speaking to former Blitz Kids now living in France, Spain, Canada, the United States and New Zealand. But there's no substitute for sitting down with someone in their living room, losing track of time over endless cups of sweet tea and mountains of biscuits.

We were often surprised at how well prepared our interviewees were for our meetings. Many opened the door to us with old photographs spread out in readiness on the kitchen table. Others had dug out wartime ration books, identity cards, telegrams, medals, or 'souvenirs' such as Henry's lump of shrapnel. Handling these tangible pieces of the past, which must lie scattered throughout cupboards, drawers and shoeboxes all over Britain, helped bring their stories to life.

The relics also served as memory aids for our interviewees. One man held his father's army medal and recalled how he had failed to recognise his dad when he came home at the end of the war. A woman showed us the reams of letters her father had written to her mother while he was in a prisoner-of-war camp, and described how devastated she had been when the missives stopped arriving.

When trying to extract memories that, in many cases, haven't surfaced for the best part of a lifetime, we've found that it's best to allow minds to meander and not to expect stories to be told in order, or even from beginning to end. As old synapses begin firing, one memory can set off another – and too many questions will break the flow. The task of making sense of it all, piecing together a timeline and a narrative, has to come later.

Sometimes, inevitably, our interviews brought up difficult emotions. But surprisingly, the tears didn't tend to come when they described houses being bombed or people dying. Far more devastating, for many of our Blitz Kids, was remembering happy times with loved ones who are no longer around. One woman remained perfectly composed while talking about the damage wrought by bombs and bullets, but both she and her son burst into tears when she told us about her much-missed late husband.

Even a book about the Blitz can't be all doom and gloom. A lot of our interviewees were riotously funny. In fact, many told us the war was a wonderful time to be a kid. With hardly any cars being driven thanks to petrol rationing, children owned the streets. Air raids opened up new areas to play in the middle of built-up cities. Bombed-out buildings became Wendy houses and adventure playgrounds. It was a time when children still had the freedom to roam, even in urban areas, and parents were largely content not knowing where they were, as long as they came home for dinner. Many of our Blitz Kids feel sorry for their grandchildren and great-grandchildren, whose childhoods are so much more restricted.

A surprising number of people we spoke to said they never felt afraid during air raids – some, apparently, even found them exciting. Could that really be true, we wondered? Had they suppressed their difficult emotions, or been told it was wrong or even unpatriotic to admit fear? One little girl was instructed not to cry during an air raid because it was 'what Hitler would have wanted'. Other children were told that the sickly feeling they felt in their tummies wasn't really fear but a reaction to the vibration of planes flying overhead.

Overwhelmingly, we were struck by how generous our Blitz Kids were, both with their time and their memories. Approaching the end of their lives, some felt a strong urge to pass on their stories before it's too late. Many of them clearly enjoyed speaking to us, talking non-stop for six hours or more. For too many older people, feeling that someone is really listening to what they have to say, and sees their life as valuable and important, is a rare experience. After we interviewed a man with terminal cancer, his wife told us on the way out that the experience had really boosted his spirits. A woman whose mother was in the early stages of dementia said it had made her feel her life was important and meaningful.

It was hard, at times, to tell people that we couldn't guarantee their stories would make it into the book. We interviewed more than eighty people but decided to focus on just fifteen stories, choosing a representative cross-section of experiences, places, ages and backgrounds – and, of course, those with the most interesting tales to tell. Inevitably for this age group, there are more women still alive than men, and the selection in the book reflects this. But we hope that, between them, the stories we have chosen provide a sense of the wide range of experiences that the war brought for children. Those we didn't manage to include, we will be gradually adding to our website: www.blitzkids.co.uk.

Spending several hours with someone, talking about their family background, their childhood, their happiest memories and their most heartbreaking moments can be a very intense experience. You get to know the person very deeply, very quickly, and at times it can feel like a therapy session. By the end of a good interview, you've formed a bond with the interviewee and saying goodbye can be a wrench.

Several Blitz Kids wouldn't let us leave before they had given us something – books or DVDs about the war, sandwiches wrapped in tin foil for the journey home, apples from their garden (along with detailed instructions for baking them), a bunch of bananas – even, in one case, a little bird ornament, which a lovely lady in Bristol gave us 'to remember her by'. It now perches on our bookshelf, next to Henry's jagged lump of shrapnel.

Gifts like these were all very much appreciated. But every one of our interviewees had already given us the greatest gift of all: their story.

1

MAUREEN

At three years old, Maureen Hunt was too young to join her brother and sister when they were evacuated from East London to Somerset, but she went to the station with her mother to wave them off.

On the platform, all the other mothers and children were in floods of tears. When Maureen looked up, she was relieved to see that her own mum wasn't crying.

'Look after your brother,' Mrs Hunt told Maureen's sister Phyllis, forcing a smile.

She turned to little Ken. 'Make sure the two of you stay together.'

She kissed them both on the cheek and they climbed aboard the train, their gas masks dangling from their shoulders. Maureen thought they looked smaller and more fragile than usual.

'Why do they have to go?' she asked her mother.

'Just to get out of London for a bit, while the war's on,' Mrs Hunt explained.

As the train began to pull away, Maureen gripped her mother's hand tightly.

'Where will they live?' she asked anxiously.

'With another family,' Mrs Hunt told her. 'In the countryside.'

At the thought of her brother and sister living with strangers, Maureen began to cry.

'But – but they won't know anybody there!' she sobbed.

'No,' said her mother gently. 'But it's the same for all the children.'

'I want to go with them!' Maureen wailed, tears streaming down her face now. 'Why can't I go with them?'

Her mother tried to explain that she wasn't old enough, but Maureen wouldn't listen. She cried all the way home, thinking of the brother and sister she had lost.

Maureen's siblings were far from the only kids leaving home for an unknown destination. Two days before Britain declared war on Germany on 3 September 1939, the government had begun Operation Pied Piper – a mass evacuation of children from London and other cities considered potential targets for air raids. Some 800,000 kids left their homes, often with no idea where in the country they were going, each carrying a stamped addressed postcard so they could write home as soon as they arrived.

In the countryside, any household with room to spare could be compelled to take in an evacuee or risk a fine, although the 'host families' were paid ten shillings and sixpence for the inconvenience.

It was left to parents to make the difficult decision of whether to send their children away or not, but in London almost half of all children were evacuated. Trains left the capital's main stations every nine minutes for nine hours a day, with thousands of members of the Women's Voluntary Service (WVS) on hand to take care of the evacuees.

With her siblings away in Somerset, Maureen was forced to adjust to her new life as an only child. The Hunts lived on Gurley Street, a stone's throw from Bromley-by-Bow Station in the London borough of Poplar. Maureen was friends with a couple of kids on the street, but she had been very close to her brother and sister, and without them around she didn't quite know what to do with herself.

The family didn't have much money, and apart from her favourite doll there were very few toys in the house. But Maureen had grown up surrounded by books, since her mother was a keen reader and made sure the shelves were well stocked. By the time Maureen was four, curling up with a good book had already become one of her favourite pastimes.

Mrs Hunt's own taste in literature was not exactly child-friendly. No one would have guessed it to meet her, but Maureen's kind and generous mother had a passion for bloodthirsty thrillers. At the cinema, she loved to watch the latest gangster flick, while her husband much preferred a Fred Astaire and Ginger Rogers movie.

Mr Hunt was a concrete leveller by trade but was semi-retired, following a workplace accident. He walked with a limp and had severe varicose veins that bulged out of his legs, and the doctor had warned him not to do any more manual labour. Now he made what money he could doing odd jobs for the council, sweeping the streets and laying down ashes when it snowed. If there was nothing going locally, he would get the bus into town and wander around all day looking for work. When war came, Mr Hunt was declared unfit for army service, but he volunteered as a fire watcher on the top of the nearby Bryant & May match factory.

Despite the difficult hand life had dealt him, Mr Hunt was permanently cheerful, and the house on Gurley Street was a happy one. The radio was on from first thing in the morning until last thing at night, and he could always be found singing along to all the latest songs. Maureen took after her father and was constantly singing and dancing.

'Perhaps she'll end up on the stage one day,' he mused, watching her performing in the back yard.

'Not if I can help it!' his wife replied. 'She'll have a proper job.'

Mrs Hunt herself had a 'proper job', working as a bookkeeper for a Jewish family called the Reubens, who owned the local fish and chip shop. Maureen went to nursery while she worked, since Mrs Hunt didn't have her own mother around any more to help look after the kids. Her father, Maureen's grandad, lived not far away but was in very bad health, having been gassed in the trenches in the last war. He had terrible chest problems and went down with bronchitis every winter without fail. Despite his breathing difficulties, he always insisted on taking Maureen out for a walk whenever he saw her. They would make their way slowly, hand in hand, stopping every few minutes when Grandad started wheezing.

As they walked around the neighbourhood, Maureen noticed strange changes taking place. All along her street, the windows had been crossed out with strips of brown tape, as if someone was playing a giant game of noughts and crosses. Up above, she saw what looked like silver elephants floating in the sky, as barrage balloons were installed along the docks to protect them from enemy aircraft.

In the Hunts' back yard there was now an Anderson shelter with a curved, corrugated iron roof covered in soil, which made Maureen think of a giant rabbit burrow. The shelters, which were provided for free to households with an income of less than £250 a year, were intended to protect families from bomb blasts and falling debris, but wouldn't be much use in the event of a direct hit.

The street lights never came on any more, and Maureen's mother had hung a set of heavy blackout curtains over the windows. If anyone mistakenly left a chink of light showing, the local Air Raid Precautions (ARP) warden came knocking on their door, ordering them to cover it up.

Londoners expected German bombs to start falling at any moment, but other than a few isolated incidents, the raids failed to materialise. By the end of the year, many children who had been evacuated at the start of the war returned home, flouting government posters warning them this was exactly what Hitler wanted them to do. But Maureen's siblings, Phyllis and Ken, remained in Somerset.

With barely any fighting taking place on the Continent, the early months of the conflict had gained the nickname the 'Phoney War'. For now, the main fight was at sea, as the Battle of the Atlantic raged. Merchant ships were torpedoed, leading to food shortages, and in January 1940 rationing had to be introduced for the first time in twenty years.

Butter, sugar, bacon and ham were the first goods to go on the ration, but for children the far more concerning changes were those which were gradually applied to chocolate and sweets. Kids over six months old were allowed two ounces of confectionary a week, and when Maureen went to the sweet shop she would agonise over how best to use her precious coupons. Sometimes she spent a good half-hour staring at the jars of liquorice allsorts and dolly mixture and bars of Cadbury's chocolate, before coming away with a little paper bag containing just a few Maltesers.

Mrs Hunt, meanwhile, was worried about the lack of fruit available at the greengrocer's, where oranges and bananas had now become a distant memory. When Maureen came out in a rash one day, the doctor told her mother it was the result of vitamin C deficiency, and urged her to give her daughter more citrus fruit. Unfortunately, the only thing Mrs Hunt could find was a lemon.

She cut it in half and handed it to Maureen. 'Suck the juice out and pretend it's an orange,' she said.

Maureen did as she was told, wincing as tears pricked her eyes.

As spring gave way to summer, the war suddenly felt much closer to home. After the fall of France and the British retreat at Dunkirk, the fight moved to the skies over southern England, as RAF Spitfires did battle with German Messerschmitts in the Battle of Britain.

When Maureen's grandad saw RAF planes flying overhead, he would raise a fist to the sky and shout, 'Go on, boys – give 'em what for!' Like most men of his generation, he was furious that the Germans had started another world war.

But for many kids, the aerial dogfights were an exciting spectacle. They enjoyed imitating the planes, running around with outstretched arms and pretending to machine-gun their friends.

Other games focused on the expected German bombing. That summer, at a play centre in Bethnal Green, nine-year-olds were observed playing at air raids. One of the girls assumed the role of Teacher, telling the others not to panic and checking that everyone had their gas masks, while the boys raced around the room screaming 'Help!' and knocking over furniture.

How kids would cope with the real thing, if and when it came, was a very different question. *Housewife* magazine reassured mothers that their little ones would likely be oblivious to the danger: 'Air raids will only mean a great noise to younger children, and provided Daddy and Mummy won't mind, they won't.'

But for older kids, they recommended a strictly rational approach: 'Reassure them by admitting the danger, but stressing the very long odds against them being hit.'

In August 1940, a number of children in London did

experience their first air raid, as the capital suffered a series of 'nuisance raids' – minor attacks used to train bomber crews and test British defences. Over the next few weeks, Londoners became used to the frequent sound of the air-raid siren, dubbed 'Wailing Winnie' or 'Moaning Minnie'. But since no intensive bombing campaign followed, before long not everyone bothered to go into the shelters when they heard it.

With her birthday approaching, Maureen's parents were more concerned about their daughter being lonely without her siblings around, so Mr Hunt decided to surprise her with an early birthday present. Knowing that she adored cats, he headed to a pet shop on the Bow Road and picked out a fluffy black kitten with a little white tuft under its chin.

He returned home and presented Maureen with her new playmate. At the sight of the tiny creature looking up at her with its big blue eyes, Maureen immediately fell in love. She took the kitten into her arms and covered its soft head with kisses.

Mr Hunt was pleased. 'What are you going to call it?' he asked.

Maureen looked at the little black fluffball in her hand. 'Dinky!' she replied, without hesitation.

A few days later, on Saturday, 7 September, Maureen was busy playing with Dinky in the back yard when the air-raid siren sounded. She watched as the neighbours, a family with twin boys, began heading into their Anderson shelter.

Maureen picked up her little kitten and ran inside. An ARP warden was hammering on the front door and Maureen's mother opened it. 'Mrs Hunt, you must get into a shelter!' the man said. 'I'd go to the one at Lusty's if I were you.'

The W. Lusty & Sons furniture factory on nearby Empson Street had a specially made concrete air-raid shelter for staff, but local people were allowed to use it too.

'Come on, love,' Maureen's mother called. 'We've got to go.'

Maureen put Dinky down, and her mother helped her on with her coat. She grabbed her favourite doll, before she and her mother ran out the door.

By the time they got to the shelter at the furniture factory, it was standing room only. It felt cold in the shelter despite all the people crowded together, and Maureen hated the concrete smell of the place. She buried her face in her mother's coat, hugging her doll tightly.

The shelter was partially underground, but nevertheless the roar of planes and the thud of bombs could soon be heard overhead. Maureen found the noises very frightening, but every time she looked up at her mother, Mrs Hunt gave her a reassuring smile.

Outside, the horror that Londoners had dreaded had finally arrived. A swarm of 348 bombers and 500 fighter planes was making its way up the Thames, heading for

East London and the docks. The first bombs fell on the Ford motor factory in Dagenham, the largest car plant in Europe, which was now producing military vehicles. The vast Beckton gasworks were also hit, leaving large areas of East London without gas. In Woolwich, the Royal Arsenal and the Siemens works were set alight, and fires raged at Harland & Wolff's North Woolwich shipyard. In East Ham, twenty-five people died when a bomb fell on a railway bridge and demolished a number of shops in the high street. The local Woolworths was flattened, trapping people in the basement underneath. In West Ham, Queen Mary's Hospital was hit, killing six patients and two nurses, while a whole family was wiped out when a Messerschmidt fighter plane crash-landed on their Anderson shelter.

The onslaught continued for over an hour, until the all clear sounded just after 6 p.m. Maureen and her mother emerged from the shelter to find the world around them a chaotic blur of smoke, flame and water. The furniture factory had been set alight by incendiary bombs and all seventeen acres of it was burning to the ground, along with 20,000 tables and chairs. Fire engines tore past with their bells ringing furiously, and enormous jets of water doused smoking, blackened shells that were barely recognisable as buildings.

Maureen's eyes stung from the heat of the fires. She felt her mother's grip on her tighten as they headed in the direction of Gurley Street, tripping over stray bricks and coughing from the smoke. Devas Street, the road before theirs, had been hit, the rows of terraced houses that had stood there less than two hours ago now gone.

As they turned the corner into their own road, Mrs Hunt gasped. Gurley Street had been completely obliterated, leaving only a smoking wasteland. All the families who had taken cover in their Anderson shelters that afternoon, including their neighbours with the twin boys, were now dead, buried beneath the scorched earth.

Maureen and her mother picked their way along slowly, scanning the rubble for any remnant of their own home. After wandering around disorientated for a while, Maureen spotted a brown leather satchel belonging to her sister, Phyllis, poking out of the debris, and realised they had found the spot where their house had once been. Maureen stood staring in disbelief, unable to comprehend that the home she knew so well had been reduced to the smouldering pile of rubble before her.

The little bag was all that remained of the family's possessions. Everything else was gone: their furniture, family photographs, the children's toys and all the books Mrs Hunt had collected for them. All they had now were the clothes on their backs and the one little doll that Maureen had been carrying.

But Maureen's only thought was for her kitten. As they surveyed the wreckage, she suddenly noticed something black and fluffy on the ground. 'Dinky!' she cried.

Before her mother could stop her, she ran over to where the little cat lay. But as she got closer, she realised something was wrong. Dinky wasn't moving, and her tiny body was twisted strangely. The beautiful blue eyes were open, but they now stared blankly from her face. Maureen burst into tears.

'Don't cry,' Mrs Hunt said, putting her arm around her daughter's shoulders. 'We'll get you another one.'

But her words didn't comfort Maureen. Nothing could ever replace Dinky.

Through her tears, she saw a figure limping towards them in the smoke.

'Daddy!' she cried.

Despite his bad leg, Mr Hunt had run all the way home from the Bryant & May factory as soon as he'd heard that Gurley Street had been hit.

'Thank God, you're all right!' he cried. He threw his arms around his wife and daughter, dizzy with relief.

They had nothing in the world now, but at least they had each other.

The Hunts headed to the local school, which had been turned into an emergency rest centre. Since Poplar was one of the boroughs worst hit in the raid, the place was packed with families who had been made homeless, many of them in a state of shock and confusion. Red Cross workers did their best to comfort them, bringing round blankets, cups of tea and sandwiches.

Maureen sat clutching her doll, so shaken by what had happened that she could barely speak. Every time she tried to say something she stuttered and couldn't seem to get the words out.

Just after 8 p.m., the siren sounded again, as a second wave of bombers arrived to drop more incendiaries and high explosives on to the already burning streets and docks. In Bermondsey, seventy-three people died, many of them when another school being used as a rest centre was bombed. In North Woolwich, the station was hit and the railway line damaged. In one of the worst incidents of the raid, a 50kg bomb dropped down a narrow ventilation shaft into a shelter in Columbia Road, Bethnal Green, containing more than 1,000 people. The blast swept babies from their prams before their mothers had a chance to protect them, and several support pillars collapsed, killing forty-five people and injuring many more. In one family, the parents survived but all three children were killed.

Fires raged in the factories and warehouses along the docks. Barrels of rum exploded like bombs, while paint, rubber, tea, sugar and soap burned, sending out clouds of black smoke so thick that firefighters could only tackle them from afar.

By the time the second all clear sounded eight hours later, a total of 649 tons of high explosives and 100,000 incendiary bombs had been dropped on London over the course of that night.

When morning broke, Mrs Hunt went to see a local friend, Mrs Godfrey, who agreed to take the family in until they could find somewhere else to live. Maureen and her parents showed up on the doorstep with not so much as a toothbrush between them, but Mrs Godfrey went out of her way to find them everything they needed.

That day, Winston Churchill came to East London to survey the damage wrought by the Luftwaffe. On visiting the site of the air-raid shelter at Colombia Road where so many families had died, he broke down in tears. 'You see, he really cares,' exclaimed one old lady.

As the crowds mobbed the prime minister, there were cries of 'We can take it, Winnie!' from the undaunted East Enders.

'Black Saturday', as it became known, turned out to be the blueprint for the eight-month bombardment that followed. Almost every night an average of 200 to 300 bombers returned, the first wave dropping incendiaries, which started fires that lit up the targets for the high-explosive bombs that followed. In the month of September, 5,730 Londoners were killed and 9,003 seriously injured. By November, in Poplar alone, 800 homes had been lost and 13,200 badly damaged.

The sustained bombing campaign soon gained a new name, taken from the German word for lightning: 'the Blitz'.

After a couple of weeks, the Hunts were allocated a new home on Devons Road – a five-minute walk from their old house on Gurley Street.

Maureen was disappointed to discover that it was just a flat above a grocer's, part of a little parade of shops on the street. Inside, it was very small, with only one bedroom, and completely unfurnished.

But Mr Hunt was undaunted. 'This'll be all right!' he said cheerfully.

They moved in straight away, sleeping on the floor since they didn't have any beds. Over the next few days, Mrs Hunt set about searching the shops for pots, pans, plates and cutlery, replacing all the essentials of everyday life that they had lost. In time, under the government's war damage to property scheme, they were able to buy some furniture too.

There was no help for families to deal with the other kinds of damage the raids had caused, however. Maureen was still so traumatised by that night that the stutter she had developed hadn't gone away. When she tried to speak, the words just wouldn't come out, and she stamped her foot in frustration.

Concerned, her mother took her to the doctor. 'It's pure nerves,' he said. 'The bombing's got to her.'

The doctor said there was nothing he could do, but Mrs Hunt wasn't going to give up so easily. She was determined to help her daughter, and whenever Maureen started to stutter, she gently encouraged her to slow down and say the sentence again. Gradually, the problem began to improve, although it always got worse when Maureen felt anxious.

Unfortunately, with the bombs falling almost every night now, Maureen was anxious much of the time. As she watched the grown-ups around her going about their business as usual, she felt as if they were all just going through the motions, pretending that normal life still existed when really all any of them were doing was surviving.

Maureen and her mother were now constantly running to the public air-raid shelter next to St Andrew's Hospital. They couldn't have set mealtimes any more, because as soon as they sat down at the table the siren would invariably go off. No one ever made any plans since they didn't know if they would be around from one day to the next. A feeling of uncertainty hung over everything.

Maureen was exhausted from all the sleepless nights, but she found she couldn't nap at nursery during the daytime. The staff were always urging the children to get as much rest as they could on their little fold-out beds, but Maureen just wasn't able to drop off. There was so much going on in the world around her, and she had so many questions.

She knew there was another country called Germany, and a man called Hitler, but she couldn't understand why they would want to drop bombs on Bromley-by-Bow every night.

'Why are they doing it to us, Mum?' she asked.

'Hitler just wants to rule the world,' was the only explanation her mother could supply.

Thankfully, the festive season brought a short reprieve from the bombing, with the Luftwaffe staying away for all of Christmas Day and Boxing Day. To Maureen's delight, her brother and sister returned from the countryside for the holidays and the whole family squeezed into the little flat on Devons Road, the children sleeping in the living room.

But the Christmas spirit didn't last. On 29 December, the Luftwaffe made up for lost time, dropping 127 tons of high explosives and 22,068 incendiaries on the City of London, in one of the worst raids so far. The resulting blaze destroyed a bigger area than the Great Fire of 1666.

Maureen had already experienced the Blitz, but for her older siblings, who had been away in the countryside, the raids were a shock to the system. Just as Maureen had developed her stutter before, the experience took a toll on the other children's nerves. Ken began sleepwalking for the first time in his life. Every night, Mrs Hunt would find him wandering about, fast asleep but with his eyes wide open. Phyllis became so anxious that one day she collapsed with a violent seizure. Her mother had to take her to hospital, where the doctors prescribed her phenobarbital.

Maureen's brother and sister soon returned to the peace and quiet of the countryside, but in Bromley-by-Bow, the Blitz continued relentlessly. A raid on 19 March 1941 saw more than 120,000 incendiaries dropped on London – the highest number to date – causing 1,881 separate fires. In Poplar alone, eighty-five people were killed, and just across the River Lea in West Ham, a fire at the Gas Light and Coke Company left eleven local authorities with no gas supply for days. Then four weeks later, on 16 April, an even heavier raid caused 2,251 fires and killed over 1,000 people.

Public buildings including the Houses of Parliament, National Gallery and St Paul's Cathedral were damaged.

On 19 April, Hitler's fifty-second birthday, the Luftwaffe celebrated with its heaviest raid yet, dropping more than 1,000 tons of high explosives for the first and only time during the Blitz, as well as 153,096 incendiaries – the largest number in any raid on Britain. Each incendiary bomb carried enough flammable material to burn for about fifteen minutes, long enough to start a nasty fire if they plunged through the roof of a house and set the attic ablaze.

One of the worst tragedies of the night occurred a short walk from Maureen's home on Devons Road, when a parachute mine hit the roof of the Old Palace School in St Leonard's Street, then being used as an auxiliary fire station. The bomb fell down the stairwell and landed in the watch room, killing two firewomen. Firemen standing in the school playground outside were caught in the blast and buried by falling masonry, as part of the building collapsed and the rest caught fire.

Some of the men were still alive and calling for help in the early hours of that morning, as rescuers tried to clear the rubble. But none of them could be reached in time. It took a week to dig out all the bodies, which piled up in a temporary mortuary on Devons Road. In all, thirty-four people died in the Old Palace School bombing, the greatest loss of Fire Brigade lives in a single incident in either war or peace.

*

Since moving into the flat on Devons Road, Maureen and her parents had been spending more time at her paternal grandmother's house, which was just a couple of minutes' walk away on Tibbatt's Road. Grandma Hunt looked like a fragile old lady, but she was an East Ender through and through, and not even falling bombs could faze her. 'We just have to get on with it the best we can,' she said matter-of-factly.

Maureen and her parents were at her house one day when the air-raid siren sounded, and they all ran into Grandma's Anderson shelter in the back yard.

When the all clear came, they said goodbye to Grandma and walked back round to Devons Road, only to find that their flat no longer existed.

The little row of shops above which they lived had been hit in the daytime raid and was now nothing more than a pile of burning rubble.

'Not again!' Maureen's mother said, staring at it in disbelief.

The shops and all their contents had gone up in flames, along with the belongings that Mrs Hunt had so painstakingly replaced after being bombed out before.

'Right, well, we'll just have to start all over again,' said Mr Hunt, undeterred as usual.

Maureen and her parents threw themselves on the mercy of her mother's friend Mrs Godfrey once more, while Mr Hunt got on to the council about getting them somewhere new to live.

The Hunts were offered a house on Old Ford Road in

Bow. When they went to see it, they were shocked at how dilapidated it was, with rainwater dripping in through several holes in the roof. But there were two decent-sized bedrooms and a box room, and it was near the lovely little Grove Hall Park. Mr Hunt could see its potential.

'I think we could make ourselves a home here,' he said confidently.

So it was that for a second time the Hunts moved house with nothing but the clothes on their backs. They got the roof fixed and Maureen's mother began her search for pots and pans all over again.

Gradually, Maureen's parents managed to make the place feel like a home, and they were even able to invite Grandad to move in with them.

On the night of 10 May, the London Blitz ended – quite literally – with a bang. It was the last attack of the eight-month bombing campaign, and for many Londoners, it was also one of the worst. Overall, Poplar sustained less damage than some of the other boroughs that night, with just 32 deaths compared to 138 in Southwark, 110 in Westminster and 87 in Camberwell – but Bow Church, less than 200 yards from Maureen's new home on Old Ford Road, took a direct hit.

The following morning, Maureen gazed up at the ruins of the bell tower, the top of which had been blasted to smithereens. Outside, the statue of Gladstone holding his hand aloft was strewn with clothes blown out of nearby houses.

Across London, the raid claimed almost 1,500 lives, the most that had ever died in one night in the city's history. More than 12,000 people were left homeless. But when it was over, the capital enjoyed a two-and-a-half-year period of peace, except for the odd minor 'tip-and-run' raid. In later years, this period of relative calm would be known as the Lull.

Over eight long months, London had been bombarded with over 18,000 tons of high explosive. More than 28,000 Londoners had been killed, and almost as many again sent to hospital with serious injuries. But now, at long last, the horrific bombing campaign had come to an end.

Phyllis and Ken were allowed to come home, and the Hunt family were finally together again. Maureen was thrilled to have her siblings back, and she and Phyllis spent all their spare time singing the American songs they'd heard on the wireless. Their favourite was 'I'll Be With You In Apple Blossom Time', and they could perform the harmonies perfectly.

To their delight, their next-door neighbour on Old Ford Road, Mr Jones, had an upright piano and could play any tune by ear. Every Sunday morning, he would play all the latest songs for them while they danced in the garden.

The Hunts' fortunes seemed to be changing. Although the fish and chip shop that Mrs Hunt worked for had been bombed out, her husband soon had a new opportunity. An old friend of his, Mr French, had been killed by a German bomb while out walking his dog, and ever since his widow had been struggling to keep their grocer's shop going.

Eventually she asked Maureen's father if he would take over the business. Mr Hunt agreed, and the sign outside was duly changed to 'Hunt's Stores'.

Maureen could see how happy her father was, welcoming all the customers each morning in his bright white coat. The shop prospered, and Mr Hunt could finally give his family all the things they had never been able to afford before. He bought Maureen dancing lessons and took her to the Mile End Odeon to see *The Wizard of Oz* five times, since they both loved it so much.

Sitting in the packed auditorium, Maureen watched entranced as the dreary black and white of Kansas gave way to glorious Technicolor. It was the most magical thing she had ever seen.

As far as Maureen was concerned, the dark days of the Blitz were far behind her.

2

KITTY

For the first twelve years of her life, Kitty Simmonds's world had been the Jewish community of Spitalfields in East London. Known as Little Jerusalem, it was full of businesses bearing signs in Yiddish and boasted the famous Petticoat Lane market, which sold kosher meat, unleavened cakes and other traditional Jewish specialities.

Kitty and her parents lived above her Uncle Yudi's dairy shop on Pelham Street, just off Brick Lane. Her father was a carpenter and had made all their furniture himself. Shortly before the war, he had lost his job making wooden surrounds for radios at the HMV factory in Hayes after taking a day off for the Jewish holy day of Yom Kippur. Now, though, he was in constant demand building army huts all over the country.

Kitty's mother helped out in her brother's shop downstairs, although more often than not she ended up running it alone. Uncle Yudi was a gambler and had no qualms about closing up early for a flutter on the horses. Small and wiry, he had once been a featherweight jockey himself but had lost his job after falling out with his manager, who had called him a 'dirty Jew'. These days, the closest he got to the races was as a spectator.

Mrs Simmonds was always fretting about Yudi. She'd already bailed him out once when the health inspector caught him diluting the milk with water. She'd had to pawn her wedding ring to pay the fine and keep her little brother out of prison.

One day, when she saw him about to shut up shop in the early afternoon, she protested, 'Think of the customers!'

'Bugger the customers!' Yudi replied, explaining he had a tip on a race that he couldn't pass up.

When he came back later flush with money, Mrs Simmonds begged him to put it in the bank. But Yudi couldn't resist placing another bet the next day, and he lost it all again when his horse broke its leg.

Kitty adored Uncle Yudi and enjoyed helping out in the shop after school. She loved patting and weighing the butter, trying to cut the exact weight the customer had asked for. But Mrs Simmonds had higher hopes for her daughter, who had already passed the scholarship exam to the Clapton County Secondary School for Girls and now travelled there each day on her own by tram.

Kitty didn't mind the journey, although sometimes she had to run rather than walk to the tram stop when one of the neighbours shouted 'Bloody Jew!' at her. Their road was split, with Jews on one side and Gentiles on the other, and antisemitism was alive and well. Three years earlier, Uncle Yudi had joined a gang of local men who fought off Oswald Mosley's fascists in the Battle of Cable Street.

At school, Kitty had become best friends with another Jewish girl called Sadie Davidovitch, although the two of them always felt like they were on the outside looking in. With Kitty's glasses and mop of unruly dark hair and Sadie's badly cut fringe, they were painfully aware they weren't as popular as girls like the pretty, blonde Sheila Foster.

In late August 1939, shortly before war was declared, Kitty's school was evacuated to rural Hertfordshire. The girls lined up in pairs outside, in their brown school uniforms, Kitty and Sadie gripping each other's hands.

Their mothers had been told not to come and see them off, but most had ignored the instruction. A gaggle of mums stood across the road from the school, and Kitty spotted her own mother among them, holding a handkerchief up to her face to hide her tears.

The form mistress told the girls to proceed quickly and quietly to Clapton Station. As they walked up the street, the mums followed along on the other side. 'Hurry up, girls!' shouted the teacher. 'And don't look over the road.'

Outside the station, Kitty and the other girls waved to their mothers and blew them kisses, tears rolling down their cheeks. Then they went inside and boarded the train.

'Do you think we'll ever see our mums again?' Kitty asked Sadie.

'Oh, Kitty,' her friend replied, throwing her arms around Kitty's neck. 'Promise me we'll always be together!'

As the train departed, the girls settled down and tried to eat the sandwiches their mothers had packed for them. But even when her stomach was full, Kitty felt empty inside.

The girls exited the train at a village called Much Hadham. With its quaint white cottages and ancient-looking pubs, it couldn't have been more different to the East End. Kitty was surprised to see no litter on the ground and no cigarette butts in the gutter.

The girls were taken to the parish hall, where they sat on long wooden benches, waiting to be picked by the locals. Kitty wasn't surprised when Sheila Foster got taken first.

One by one, the other girls were chosen, until Kitty and Sadie were left alone on the bench. Tears pricked Kitty's eyes behind her glasses.

Eventually a young couple arrived and, to the girls' great relief, agreed to take the two of them together. They lived in a little cottage a few miles outside the village, in a remote spot that was far from the nearest neighbour. Kitty and Sadie couldn't help feeling there was something spooky about the place. It didn't help that the downstairs was lit by a single paraffin lamp, which cast strange shadows all over the walls.

That night, lying on mattresses on the bare wooden floor, the two girls cried themselves to sleep.

The next morning, they woke to find the young couple staring down at them.

'What is it?' Kitty asked, sitting up quickly.

'We're just looking for the horns,' the man replied.

The girls, he explained, were the first Jews he and his wife had ever met. He wanted to know if it was true, as he had heard, that they had horns on their heads.

Kitty couldn't believe what she was hearing. 'That's daft!' she exclaimed. 'We're just the same as everybody else.'

She and Sadie began to laugh, and after a few moments the young couple joined in too, reassured that their houseguests were not in fact horned devils. Then the four of them settled down to a friendly breakfast together.

Despite their strange ideas, the young couple turned out to be kind and attentive hosts, so it was with mixed feelings that Kitty and Sadie learned they would soon be on the move again. Their headmistress hadn't been able to find a building suitable for a school in Much Hadham, so they were heading to the nearby market town of Bishop's Stortford instead. A school there had offered to let the evacuees use its classrooms in the afternoons, while its own pupils would take their lessons in the mornings.

Once again, Kitty and Sadie found themselves seated on a cold wooden bench, waiting to be chosen by the locals. Again, Sheila Foster was the first to be picked and they were almost last.

This time, it was an older, well-to-do couple who claimed them. The woman introduced herself as Mrs Barker and leaned in to inspect the girls' name tags.

'*Davidovitch?*' she remarked, peering at Sadie's tag. 'That's not an English name. Where are you from?'

'I'm from London,' Sadie answered awkwardly.

Mr and Mrs Barker led the girls outside and ushered them into a large car, smarter than any Kitty had been in before. Their home, it turned out, was equally grand, with brass stair rods on every step of the carpeted staircase and a large bowl of flowers on a table in the hallway. Compared to the cramped flat above the dairy shop, it felt like a palace.

The next day was Sunday, and the girls awoke to find the table already laid for breakfast. 'Eat up!' Mrs Barker instructed them. 'We'll be late for church.'

Kitty and Sadie exchanged glances.

'We can't go to church,' Kitty said. 'We're Jewish.'

'Jewish?' Mrs Barker exclaimed. 'They didn't tell us *that*.'

She thought for a moment. 'Well, I suppose you can stay at home and get things ready for lunch.'

While the Barkers went out to church, Kitty and Sadie tidied up the kitchen and washed and dried the dishes. But they soon discovered a new problem. Mrs Barker had left the Sunday roast in the oven, and it definitely wasn't kosher.

'What are we going to do about the meat?' Kitty asked.

'We'll just eat the greens and potatoes,' Sadie suggested. 'If there's a sweet too, that'll be enough.'

But when Kitty explained their dietary restrictions to Mrs Barker, their hostess was less than sympathetic. 'Not eat the meat?' she retorted. 'You'll not waste good food in my house!'

'We'll eat everything else,' Sadie pleaded. 'We don't want to be difficult.'

'Look, girls,' Mr Barker said crossly. 'We took you in to save you from the bombs. When you're in our house, you'll eat what we eat!'

But Kitty was adamant. 'No!' she replied. 'We just *can't*.'

She and Sadie stuck to their guns, and the rest of the meal passed in strained silence.

Later that day, Mrs Barker told the girls they should use the back door to the house in future. 'The front door is for guests only,' she said coolly.

The girls duly began using the servants' entrance, and as time went on, that was increasingly how their hostess made them feel. Since they only went to school in the afternoons, she soon began finding chores to keep them occupied in the mornings.

It started with sweeping the kitchen floor but soon progressed to cleaning the entire kitchen every day, and then the dining room too. 'Be careful with the ornaments,' Mrs Barker warned. 'If you break any, you'll have to replace them.'

Before long, the girls had become a pair of domestic drudges, their fingers grimy from all the dirty work and their knees sore from crawling around polishing the floors.

Even Mr Barker protested when he saw all the chores his wife had given them. 'We said we'd take them in, not make them char for us,' he told her.

'Well, they can pay their way,' his wife replied.

But Kitty had soon had enough of being treated as a skivvy. The next time she penned a letter to her mother back in London, she told her what was going on. 'I hate it!' she wrote. 'We have to get up so early to get everything done before lunch. I *so* want to come home, and Sadie feels the same.'

A few days later, the girls were polishing the floor in the hallway when they heard a knock at the front door. It was Kitty's mother, come all the way from London.

Kitty was so overjoyed to see her that she almost tripped as she ran to give her a hug. But when Mrs Simmonds saw her daughter's filthy apron and the state of her scraped, bruised knees, tears welled up in her eyes.

'How can you take advantage of children like this?' she asked Mrs Barker. 'I think I'd better speak to the girls' headmistress!'

'Please don't do that!' Mrs Barker begged. 'I'll get a charwoman instead.'

After several cups of tea and repeated promises to treat the girls better, Mrs Barker managed to mollify Kitty's mother. Eventually, Mrs Simmonds agreed not to broach the matter with the school, and she went back to London on the train.

Kitty was sad to see her mother go, but at least Mrs Barker had sworn there would be no more cleaning. However, as soon as the dust started settling on their hostess's fancy knick-knacks, her promises evaporated and the girls were transformed into skivvies again.

This time, Kitty found a more creative outlet for her resentment. She sat down and wrote a song about Mrs Barker and her endless chores, jotting down the lyrics on a scrap of paper, before performing it for Sadie's entertainment.

'She's such a blinking old cow,' Kitty sang. 'A stingy miser too! While we are doing all her work, she hasn't anything to do.'

Sadie giggled. 'You'd better hide that!'

Kitty put the song in her satchel and forgot all about it. But a few days later, she was summoned to the headmistress's office.

Dr Hunt was a tall, thin woman, who wore her hair in a neat bun on the top of her head. 'Kitty, Mrs Barker was here this morning,' she said, passing a piece of paper across the desk.

Kitty realised with horror that it was her song.

'Is this yours?' the headmistress demanded.

Kitty fumed. What right did Mrs Barker have to go through her bag? But there was no point denying it now. 'Yes,' she admitted. 'I wrote it.'

She told Dr Hunt all about the chores she and Sadie had been forced to do around the house, and how their hostess had turned them into skivvies. To her surprise, the headmistress was unsympathetic. 'You have no right to call Mrs Barker names,' she told Kitty sternly. 'If we were in London now, I would suspend you.'

As it was, Kitty was landed with 500 lines instead: *I must respect my elders and not be rude to people who are kind to me.* Every time she wrote the words out, she felt more and more resentful. But worse still, she was ordered to apologise to Mrs Barker.

Kitty was too angry to speak to her hostess that evening. When Mrs Barker called the girls down for tea, Sadie did as she was told, while Kitty remained stubbornly in her room.

A few minutes later, Mrs Barker marched up the stairs, red-faced. 'Kitty! Come down *now*!' she demanded.

'No,' Kitty replied. 'I don't want your tea. I hate you!' Then she burst into tears.

'You ungrateful child!' Mrs Barker said. 'Sadie would never speak to me like that.'

'Sadie has no guts!' Kitty shot back.

Mrs Barker slammed the door and stormed back downstairs.

By the time Sadie returned to their room, Kitty had come up with a plan. 'Why don't we run away?' she suggested.

'We can't!' protested Sadie. 'Our mums would kill us, and so would Dr Hunt. I hate it here too, but there's nothing we can do.'

Kitty wasn't easily dissuaded, however. The following morning at breakfast she greeted Mrs Barker as if nothing had happened. Then she and Sadie did their chores before setting off for school. On the way, Kitty stopped suddenly, telling her friend she'd forgotten her homework and would have to go back for it. 'You go on ahead,' she told Sadie.

Kitty didn't return to the Barker house. Instead, she made her way to the train station, where she asked to buy a ticket to London. Her mother had recently sent her some pocket money, which was just about enough to cover the fare.

The ticket clerk peered at her suspiciously. 'A girl your age shouldn't be taking trains by herself,' he said.

'My mum's meeting me at the other end,' Kitty lied. 'My dad's home on leave so she sent me the money for the train.'

The man looked doubtful, but he sold her the ticket anyway, and soon Kitty was on her way back home.

'What are you doing here?' Mrs Simmonds cried when her daughter walked through the door of the dairy shop. 'You're supposed to be in the country!' She ran over and hugged Kitty tightly, then ushered her into the kitchen at the back of the shop.

Uncle Yudi was busy toasting a piece of bread on the end of a fork. When he saw Kitty he was so startled that he dropped it in the fire.

'This is a nice surprise!' he grinned. 'Life's been very quiet here without you, girl.'

'Does the school know you're home, Kitty?' Mrs Simmonds asked anxiously.

'No,' Kitty admitted. 'And neither does anyone else. But I'm not going back!'

'Oh, Kitty!' her mother exclaimed. 'Mrs Barker must be worried out of her wits. I'm sure they'll call the police!'

Uncle Yudi put his hand on his sister's shoulder. 'Take some coppers from the till and call Mrs Barker,' he told her. 'Let her know Kitty's safe.'

While Mrs Simmonds hurried off to make the call, Yudi turned to his niece. 'Now, girl, tell me why you really came home,' he said. 'Did you steal something?'

'No!' replied Kitty indignantly. She sat down and told him the whole story from beginning to end, including the bit about the rude song she had written.

A smile spread across Yudi's face. 'You take after your uncle!' he chuckled. 'But your mum'll go mad when she finds out.'

He thought for a moment. 'You'd better go upstairs. I'll tell her you felt sick and went to bed.'

Kitty thanked him and ran gratefully to her room.

The following morning, Kitty's mother told her she would have to go back to Bishop's Stortford right away.

Kitty pulled the covers over her head. 'I'm not going back to Mrs Barker's!' she cried.

Mrs Simmonds begged and cajoled, but her daughter refused to budge. Eventually, she phoned Kitty's headmistress, who agreed to find a new family for her to stay with.

'Will you go back now, for my sake?' she pleaded. 'I don't want anything to happen to you here.'

Looking at her mother's anxious face, Kitty agreed to give evacuation another go.

This time, she was sent to live with a family who had a daughter her own age, in an even grander house on the opposite side of town. But it turned out to be no better than the Barkers'. Kitty wasn't allowed to eat with the family and had to take her meals in the kitchen with the servants. When she tried to enter the living room, the hosts' daughter told her haughtily, 'You shouldn't be in here. You come from the slums of London.'

That night, Kitty felt lonelier than she ever had in her life.

At least back at school she could see Sadie again. Her friend came over and hugged her. 'I'm so glad to see you!' she cried. 'I was so upset when you ran away.'

She told Kitty that Mrs Barker was still making her do the housework, although not as much as before, and that she was 'trying to be nice'.

Back at Kitty's own billet, things remained as frosty as ever. After two weeks, she couldn't stand it any more and decided to pull another disappearing act. She left a note for her headmistress this time, so no one could accuse her of causing unnecessary worry, and then set off for the train station. A few hours later she was back in the East End.

It was the Sabbath, so the dairy shop was closed, but there was a light on in the kitchen at the back.

Kitty knocked, and her mother came to the door. 'Kitty!' she shrieked. 'What are you doing here?'

'I've come home to stay,' Kitty told her. 'I'm not going back.'

Mrs Simmonds put her arms around her daughter and began to cry. 'I just want you safe, Kitty,' she sobbed. 'Who knows when the raids will start?'

But Kitty wasn't worried about that. All she knew was that she was back at home, where she belonged, and it felt wonderful.

The next morning, she asked Uncle Yudi to help convince her mother to let her stay.

'I'll work on your mum,' he reassured her. 'You know how she hates to see you cry, so you just turn on the water-works and between us we'll keep you here!'

With her uncle's help, Kitty gradually wore her mother down, until eventually she agreed to call the headmistress and tell her that Kitty would be staying in London for good.

'I don't know what we'll do about your education,' Mrs Simmonds sighed.

But Kitty and Yudi already had an answer. Kitty would continue her studies at the local library and at nearby Toynbee Hall, which had just started offering classes for children who had returned from evacuation. Meanwhile, her uncle would tutor her in maths. As an experienced gambler, Yudi had an excellent grasp of figures.

To begin with, since the so-called Phoney War was still on, Kitty's decision to stay in London didn't cause her mother too much worry. But when the first nuisance raids began in the summer of 1940, Mrs Simmonds became increasingly anxious.

As soon as the siren sounded, she would shake Kitty awake and drag her to the shelter in the crypt of a nearby church. Uncle Yudi refused point-blank to go with them, declaring that he would take his chances in the flat above the dairy shop – or, more often than not, the local pub.

Soon, he wasn't the only one who refused to take the sirens seriously. Kitty began to resent being hauled out of bed in the night, and now, when her mother came to get her, she would roll over and pretend to be asleep. But this only made Mrs Simmonds more panicked. 'Come *on*, Kitty!' she would cry, pulling the covers off her daughter.

On Black Saturday, when the bombers finally came to London in force, Kitty and her mother were out window-shopping in Whitechapel. The siren sounded just as they passed the Lyons tea room, and air-raid wardens began blowing their whistles and telling people to take cover.

Kitty and her mother followed the crowd into Whitechapel Station. Since it wasn't very deep, they could hear the drone of the enemy planes overhead and the whoosh and crash of the bombs as they fell. Kitty was fascinated and decided to go and have a look, but an air-raid warden stopped her. 'Get back!' he shouted, pushing her away.

Kitty stumbled back into her mother's arms and Mrs Simmonds held her tightly.

As the onslaught continued, the lights in the station began to flicker. Kitty could feel her mother trembling.

In less than an hour the all clear sounded, and the crowd surged back up to the street. There was no visible damage in Whitechapel, but the sky was black with smoke. An air-raid warden told them it was coming from the docks.

'We must find Yudi!' cried Mrs Simmonds. 'I only hope he's still alive.'

'Mum, they said it was the docks,' Kitty reassured her. 'Our house is the other way.'

But Mrs Simmonds wasn't listening. She was too busy hurrying home.

When they got back to Pelham Street, the dairy shop was still there, looking exactly as it always did. Inside, Uncle Yudi was enjoying a cup of tea.

'What are you so worried for?' he asked, seeing the anxious look on his sister's face. 'I told you everything'd be all right!'

By the time the bombers returned two hours later, Kitty and her mother had already gone to bed. Mrs Simmonds jumped up and searched frantically for her glasses, not realising she had fallen asleep with them on the end of her nose.

Kitty tried to turn over and go back to sleep, but her uncle came and told her to get up. 'Go with your mum, or she'll have a fit,' he urged her. 'You know how bloomin' frightened she is.'

With a sigh, Kitty did as she was told, throwing a coat over her nightie and running to the shelter with her mother. Inside the crypt, most of their neighbours were already sitting on benches in their nightclothes.

Kitty could hear explosions outside, but they didn't sound too close. She lay down with her head in her mother's lap and fell asleep.

When she awoke, it was 5 a.m. and the all clear had just sounded. Everyone shuffled out of the shelter, stretching and rubbing their eyes. Once again, columns of black smoke were rising from the docks.

Kitty and her mother walked quickly back around the corner to the dairy shop. 'Yudi! *Yudi!*' called Mrs Simmonds, running up the stairs.

But all that came from Uncle Yudi's room was the sound of snoring. Like his niece, he had somehow managed to sleep through the first night of the Blitz.

From then on, as the raids continued night after night, so too did the battle between Kitty and her mother. Kitty hated going down to the shelter and didn't see why she should have to do it when her uncle didn't. Yudi always said that if a bomb had your number on it, it would get you, so there was no point running.

But every time Kitty tried to argue, Mrs Simmonds got so worked up she started screaming at her. In the end, Kitty would always be forced to go.

After the crypt was put off-limits by an unexploded bomb, they began spending their nights in the cellar of Truman's Brewery instead. When that got bombed too, they started using Spitalfields Fruit Exchange, even though it stank of rotten fruit and vegetables, which made Kitty feel sick.

One Saturday evening they turned up there, only to find it was full. Kitty's mother started to cry.

'Let's go home,' Kitty told her. 'I can't hear any planes anyway.'

'No!' Mrs Simmonds wailed. 'It'll start soon!'

Some other mothers and children who hadn't managed to get into the shelter were heading for Liverpool Street Tube Station, so Kitty and her mother followed them.

To begin with, the government had tried to prevent people using the Underground network during air raids, concerned at the risk of so many people congregating in close proximity. But the East Enders had persisted, and by the end of September, fifteen miles of platforms and tunnels had been officially opened to the public, enough to accommodate more than 150,000 people.

When Kitty and her mother arrived at the station, it was so crowded that people were sleeping not just on the platforms but on the escalators as well. They decided to take a train one stop to Bank, but that also turned out to be full.

Mrs Simmonds began to cry again. 'What are we going to do?' she wailed.

'Try the next one,' a man on the platform told her.

Kitty and her mother hopped on the Tube again, this time to St Paul's. There, they picked their way along the platform, looking for a spot to lay their blankets.

Eventually, they found somewhere, but Kitty struggled to sleep on the cold, hard platform with the sound of the trains rushing past and the smell of sweaty people all around.

Yet to her horror, her mother thought the Tube was the ideal shelter, and from that evening on she insisted they go down there every night.

As the months went by, Kitty got more and more fed up with going into the Underground and struggling to sleep on the crowded, smelly platform. Uncle Yudi still spent all his evenings at home or in the pub, and yet the fabled bomb with his number on it never seemed to find him. Kitty grew used to the sight of bomb-damaged buildings in the mornings and overhearing hushed conversations about those who had been lost in the raids, but since she rarely knew any of the people who were killed personally, it never felt like the bombs were intended for her.

After half a year of more or less continuous bombing, the Blitz had become drearily routine. So much so that one evening, in the spring of 1941, Kitty declared she'd had enough. 'I'm *not* going tonight,' she told her mum defiantly, when Mrs Simmonds instructed her to get ready.

Kitty's mother was in the middle of frying some fish-cakes to take with them, and when she heard Kitty's words, she began to tremble. 'Do you want us to be killed?' she cried desperately.

'No, Mum,' replied Kitty. 'But like Uncle Yudi said . . .'

'Uncle Yudi is *stupid*!' Mrs Simmonds shouted. 'I prom-ised your dad I'd keep you safe while he was away. You'll come with me, and you'll come now!'

But Kitty was immovable. 'I'm *not* going!' she repeated.

Kitty thought her mother was about to cry, but instead Mrs Simmonds raised the spatula and hurled a fishcake across the room at her. It hit the wall just inches from Kitty's head, splattering hot oil all over the wallpaper.

Kitty burst into tears. 'I don't *want* to go, Mummy,' she sobbed. 'Please don't make me.'

Her mother rushed over and threw her arms around her, tears streaming down her face too now. 'I'm so sorry, Kitty,' she said. 'I didn't mean to hurt you.'

Mrs Simmonds looked utterly exhausted, and suddenly Kitty felt sorry for her. She allowed herself to be led up the stairs to her bedroom and dressed in warm clothes. Then the two of them set out for Liverpool Street Station.

It was already getting dark, and Kitty could barely keep up with her mother as she hurried along the road. But when Mrs Simmonds heard the siren begin to wail, she stopped, frozen with fear. 'I told you we should have started out earlier!' she cried.

Moments later the first bombs began to fall. Kitty could hear the explosions, far off at first but getting closer by the second. 'Come *on*, Mum!' she said. But her mother was rooted to the spot.

People all around them were racing up the road in search of shelter. Kitty tried to pull her mother forward.

'We have to run!' she shouted, as a nearby anti-aircraft gun opened fire.

But Mrs Simmonds wouldn't budge.

'Help!' Kitty screamed. '*Help!*' She had never felt so terrified in her life.

An air-raid warden rushed over to them. 'What's the matter?' he asked.

'It's my mum – she won't move!' Kitty replied.

'I promised my husband I'd look after her, and now she's going to get killed!' Mrs Simmonds cried.

'Stop this, madam!' the warden shouted. 'You have to run!'

He slapped Kitty's mother hard across the face. The sudden shock seemed to snap her out of her stupor.

'*Run!*' he repeated. Kitty and her mother began racing up the road.

At last, they reached Liverpool Street Station. Kitty led her mum down to the platform, and they took the train two stops to St Paul's. Once they were safely on the platform, Mrs Simmonds began to recover her senses.

Kitty, too, saw things more clearly than she had before. That night she had been the one terrified of losing someone she loved, and finally she could understand her mother's fear.

From then on, she decided, she would never argue with her about going down to the Tube again.

On the night of 10 May 1941, Kitty and her mother were in their usual spot on the platform. Up above them, the air raid sounded worse than ever, and now and then men would rush up the escalators to find out what was going on at street level.

'A milk bar across the road just got it,' one of them said grimly when he returned. Kitty thought she could make out the sound of the ambulance sirens as the injured were carted off to hospital.

Then, suddenly, the lights in the station went out, plunging them all into darkness. Kitty gripped her mother tightly.

After a while, someone started to sing 'It's down, down in the underground . . .' Before long, others joined in. Eventually, Kitty drifted off to sleep.

When the all clear sounded just before 6 a.m., she and her mother made their way up the escalators to begin the mile-and-a-half walk home. As soon as they exited the station, they were hit with the acrid smell of smoke. Kitty caught a glimpse of the ruined milk bar opposite the station and wondered how many people had been in it when the bombs fell.

'I hope Uncle Yudi's all right,' her mother fretted, as they made their way along Cheapside, past the smouldering ruins of St Mary-le-Bow church, whose famous bells were said to mark out the territory of the Cockneys. Now Christopher Wren's magnificent steeple was pretty much all that was left of the building.

St Mary-le-Bow was far from the only London icon that had met a fiery fate in the night. The chamber of the House of Commons had also been engulfed in flames, reducing the speaker's chair to a pile of ash. The roof of Westminster Abbey was gone, the Old Bailey had lost every one of its windows, and at the British Museum Library more than 250,000 precious books had been destroyed.

It was only thanks to the tireless work of London's fire crews that St Paul's Cathedral hadn't so far succumbed to the flames. The Salvation Army headquarters on nearby Queen Victoria Street had collapsed in a towering inferno, and fires were still raging on both sides of the road. If the flames reached the ancient College of Arms on the north side, there would be nothing to stop them racing a hundred yards up Godliman Street and engulfing St Paul's as well. If that happened, the fire service had orders to create a firebreak by blowing up the road with dynamite.

As Kitty and her mother made their way home that morning, many of the 2,000-odd fires started the night before were still burning, and it wasn't until mid-afternoon that the worst of them came under control. In the City, the smoke they gave off was mixing with the stench of raw sewage coming from a fractured pipe, creating even more noxious smells than usual.

When the two of them got closer to home, they saw many residential properties had also been wiped out, leaving nothing more than rubble – or in some cases, just a bare staircase reaching towards the sky. With almost a thousand London roads now closed off by the authorities, they had to adapt their route several times, but eventually they made it to the top of Pelham Street.

Near the junction with Brick Lane, the damage didn't look too bad, but the closer they got to home the worse it was. Kitty spotted Uncle Yudi standing in the street outside the dairy shop, surrounded by a scene of devastation. A bomb had landed just behind the shop, blowing out all the windows in the building and leaving the brickwork riddled with holes. The blast had sent the family's belongings flying into the street. Kitty could see one of her father's jackets, still on its hanger, pinned to a wall, while sheet music from their piano was scattered across the pavement.

But she and her mother were only concerned for Uncle Yudi. 'Thank God you're alive!' Mrs Simmonds exclaimed, rushing up to embrace him. 'Were you at home when it happened?'

'What do you think?' Yudi replied cheerfully, gesturing at the bomb-damaged building. 'I was in the pub!'

Yudi's fondness for a drink had evidently saved his life, even if he had lost his home and business. The dairy shop and the flat above it were both deemed unsafe and were soon boarded up by the authorities.

Kitty, her mum and Uncle Yudi headed to the local rest centre, which was in Kitty's old infant school. It was noisy and smelled almost as bad as the Tube, but at least the camp beds there were an improvement on the hard Tube platform.

With nowhere else to go, the family stayed at the rest centre for several weeks, while they waited for the council to rehouse them. At last they were offered a house just a few streets away from the old dairy shop.

KITTY

The raid that had destroyed the shop turned out to be the last one of the Blitz. Somehow, despite Kitty's best efforts, Mrs Simmonds had done what she promised her husband. She had managed to keep their daughter safe.

3

ROBERT

Robert Wickens was five years old when the bombs first fell on London. His father was a merchant sailor, and the family lived in a block of flats on Manisty Street, Poplar, a stone's throw from the docks. These days, Mr Wickens was barely ever at home, since he was busy dodging German U-boats on the route between Britain and America.

Robert had only one sibling, a sister called Mary, who was twenty years older than him. Mary was the result of Mrs Wickens's first marriage, but she had never known her father since he had been killed at the Somme in 1916. Luckily, Mr Wickens had taken to the little girl straight away and had brought her up as his own.

Mary's parentage was an open secret, but little did Robert know that another, much more shameful secret hung over his own. The fear that it might be revealed by some local busybody or other had already been the cause of several sudden house moves during his young life.

Robert's mother and sister both worked in the West End, at the famous Lyons Corner House on the Strand. Mary was a 'nippy', waiting tables in the traditional black-and-white uniform with Peter Pan collar and pearl buttons, while Mrs Wickens worked behind the scenes as a cook.

When his mother and older sister were out at work, Robert was left in the care of a woman called Mrs Yates. Her husband was a painter and decorator, and they lived half a mile away near Pennyfields, in the heart of London's original Chinatown. Robert enjoyed walking along the bustling streets with Mrs Yates, peering through the windows of the local restaurants with their crispy Peking ducks strung up inside.

The Yateses lived next to a Chinese restaurant themselves, but it would never have occurred to them to eat there. The only time they sampled its wares was when one of the live ducks escaped from its back yard and found its way into their garden. Mrs Yates reached for the axe her husband used for chopping firewood, and with one swift blow cut the duck's head clean off.

Little Robert watched in amazement as the headless bird began running around in circles before bolting down the side passage and into the road.

Mrs Yates gave chase, determined not to let a free lunch get away. She eventually caught up with her quarry, returning home victorious with the bird dangling by its feet.

A few hours later she was serving up a delicious dinner of roast duck and Yorkshire pudding – with no soy sauce in sight.

*

Robert's favourite place to go with Mrs Yates was the rec-reation ground on the East India Dock Road. There, he would gaze at the statue of an angel that commemorated eighteen children killed when a bomb hit a local primary school in the previous war. Most of the dead had been between four and six years old – around the same age as he was now.

When the German planes returned to Poplar in the autumn of 1940, local children found themselves in the firing line once again. Robert now spent his nights with his mother and his sister Mary in the cellar of their block of flats, listening to the crump of bombs overhead.

In the mornings he would rush out to comb the streets for 'souvenirs', such as pieces of shrapnel, tail fins from incendiary bombs and bits of parachute mines. Before long he had amassed quite a collection, which he proudly displayed in a little glass cabinet.

One day Robert was searching the rubble as usual when he came across a large piece from a naval mine. It was too heavy to carry, so he ran home and got his toy wheelbarrow. With a bit of effort, he managed to get the chunk of metal into it and trundled it back along the road.

Before he reached his block of flats, a stranger came up to him. 'Where are you taking that, son?' he asked.

'I'm taking it home,' Robert told him.

'Have you got any more like that?'

'Yes,' Robert replied innocently. 'I've got lots!'

The stranger seemed impressed and asked Robert for his address, which the little boy happily gave him.

Later that day, there was a knock at the door. Mrs Wickens opened it to find a bomb disposal team waiting on her doorstep.

Robert watched in horror as the men marched inside, seized his entire collection of souvenirs and confiscated them. He was devastated.

There was no time for him to rebuild his collection, however. The Wickenses were about to set off for the annual 'Londoners' holiday' in the hop fields of Kent. Every year, tens of thousands of women and children from the East End would flee the city to help with the harvest. If they could strip the bines quickly enough, there was decent money to be made, and for the kids growing up in smoggy London, the health benefits of a few weeks in the countryside more than outweighed the missed schooling.

For many London families, hopping was the closest they ever came to an actual holiday. And in 1940, with the East End suffering nightly visits from the Luftwaffe, the appeal of the 'Garden of England' was greater than ever.

Early one morning, Robert, Mary and their mother caught the Hoppers' Special from London Bridge to Goudhurst in Kent. The train was packed with families like their own, each of them dragging a bulky 'hopping box' along with them. These wooden tea chests were filled with everything a family might need while living in a hut in a field for several weeks, from huge cast-iron 'hopping pots' for cooking over an open fire to empty palliasses that could be stuffed with straw and slept on. Some house-proud hoppers even brought ornaments and soft furnishings along with them. The hopping box itself doubled as the family's dining table and was also a convenient place to hide small children from ticket inspectors to save on the cost of the train journey.

For little Robert, life in the hop fields was idyllic. While the women toiled, he was free to roam, playing games and swinging on the vines with the other London kids. At the end of each day, a cry of 'Pull no more bines' rang out across the fields, and the families returned to their huts. Mrs Wickens lit a faggot fire outside and cooked up a hearty stew in her hopping pot. As the light faded, the sickly smell of hops gave way to more appealing aromas, as all the other mothers did the same.

Then the singalongs began – a mixture of East End favourites, such as 'Roll Out the Barrel' and 'Knees Up Mother Brown', and traditional hopping songs including 'My Lovely Hops' and the popular 'Hopping Down in Kent':

> *Oh, they say hopping's lousy,*
> *I don't believe it's true.*
> *We only go down hopping*
> *To earn a bob or two.*

The adults would sit out nattering late into the evening, while the kids took themselves off to bed. After a day in the fresh country air, Robert always slept soundly.

But even far from London, the Wickenses couldn't escape the war altogether. In the skies above them the Battle of Britain was reaching its climax, and Robert and the other kids watched excitedly as daring dogfights took place overhead. Mrs Wickens, whose first husband had been killed by the Germans, always cheered on the British planes and hurled abuse at the enemy ones.

One day, Robert watched in astonishment as a German aircraft was shot down and crash-landed just across the road from the hop field. The pilot struggled out of the wreckage, cut and bloodied from the crash. But before he could get to his feet, some of the men who worked as pole-pullers on the vines ran over and grabbed him. They began beating him up, kicking and punching him mercilessly.

The women and children rushed over. All the mothers were outraged at what they saw. 'Leave him alone!' they cried. 'He's wounded!'

To Robert's surprise, even his own mother, who detested the Germans, joined in with their pleas.

The women's words had the desired effect, and the men reluctantly left the German pilot alone. He was turned over to the Home Guard and taken away as an official POW.

Despite herself, Mrs Wickens had helped save a German's life that day.

Robert was expecting to go back to London at the end of hop-picking season, but one day the family received news that their block of flats had been hit in an air raid. The bomb had fallen at the far end of the building, but it had left the entire block structurally unsound and they would not be able to return there. Mrs Wickens went up to London to arrange for the family's furniture to be put into storage.

When the hop harvest was over, the other East Enders prepared to go home. But Mrs Wickens decided that they would remain in Kent, and she and Mary would find work as farm labourers. Even after the picking was over there was plenty of work to do – the hops had to be laid out and dried over beds of charcoal in the oasthouse, and new vines trained to grow up lengths of string in the fields, ready for the following year.

To begin with, the family rented an old wooden cara-van in the garden of a nearby cottage. Its owner was an old lady who turned out to be something of an eccentric. She kept a herd of pet goats, and while Robert and his family were consigned to the garden, the animals had free run of her house. The few times Mrs Wickens had occasion to go inside, she returned complaining that it stank to high heaven.

Before long, Mrs Wickens moved them into a little cot-tage of their own in nearby Horsmonden, but it was only a marginal improvement. The place had no electricity or running water, and the 'toilet' was a bucket that had to be taken down to the end of the garden each day. Robert was given the job of digging a hole, while Mary was charged with pouring in the slops.

Eventually, they moved into a more modern bunga-low owned by a local farmer. The house next door was occupied by the farm's foreman, Mr Giles, and his family. Two of the six Giles children, Margaret and Tommy, were around Robert's age, and he soon became firm friends with them.

Unfortunately, not everyone in Kent was as welcoming. While the locals were familiar with Londoners thanks to the annual influx of hop-pickers, for the most part they tolerated rather than embraced them. Shopkeepers kept their produce behind chicken wire during hopping season, believing all Cockneys to be thieves, and put up signs instructing only two 'foreigners' (their word for Londoners) to come inside at any one time. Some pubs refused to serve the visitors altogether or would only do so via a hatch in the wall.

Unsurprisingly, such attitudes filtered down to the local children. When Robert joined the village school, he found himself the only 'foreigner' in a class of Kentish kids, and a target for bullies. One day he was walking home when two bigger boys began following him, taunting him about his accent and calling him a 'dirty Cockney'. The taunts soon progressed to punches, and before long Robert was getting a good beating.

It was two against one, and Robert knew he stood little chance against the bullies. But as luck would have it an old lady happened to walk down the footpath towards them. Robert saw an opportunity to escape. 'Grandma!' he shouted.

The two boys stopped dead in their tracks and Robert was able to break away and run towards the old lady. She stared at him in confusion as he carried on running straight past her and belted all the way home.

When he got back, Mrs Wickens insisted on taking the matter up with the police. But the village bobby, an old man who had been dragged out of retirement thanks to the war, refused to help. When they went to speak to Robert's headmaster, he was equally uninterested. Thankfully, after their run-in with 'Grandma', the two boys didn't bother Robert again.

Other than that, life in Kent wasn't too bad. Robert had his friends next door, while his sister, Mary, had found herself a boyfriend. He was an army driver by the name of Maurice, whom she'd met while working shifts at the Eight Bells pub in Goudhurst. His colonel liked drinking in the pub, and when he did, Maurice whiled away the hours chatting to the pretty barmaid.

Before long, wedding bells were in the air. Mary and Maurice were married at the registry office in Cranbrook, and soon the couple announced they were expecting a baby.

When little Barbara was born, Robert was thrilled. Since Mary was so much older than him, he had often felt a bit like an only child, but he and Barbara were close enough in age that it was like having a baby sister.

Robert would have been content to stay in Kent forever, but fate soon intervened. Their neighbour, Mr Giles, suffered a heart attack and died, leaving Robert's friends next door fatherless. The farmer had to hire a new foreman, and since he didn't feel able to turf out Mr Giles's widow and six children, the Wickenses were asked to vacate their bungalow instead. With great sadness, Robert said good-bye to his friends.

By now the Blitz on London was over, but the Wickenses didn't go back to Poplar right away. Instead, they went to stay by the docks in Seaforth, just north of Liverpool, where Mr Wickens's ship was due to arrive any time soon. Robert steeled himself for the 300-mile journey, preparing to feel like a 'foreigner' once again in a place even further away from the East End.

But adjusting to life up on Merseyside proved easier than he expected. When he started at the local Catholic school, Robert found the kids there far more friendly than the Kentish children. Liverpool, Robert realised, had more in common with Poplar than Kent did. Living near the docks in Seaforth, the kids were used to sailors arriving from all over the world, and they didn't bat an eyelid at his London accent. Difference was just a part of daily life, not something to be scared of.

Mr Wickens returned from his voyage to New York smartly dressed, in a new black suit and homburg hat. He came bearing gifts for the whole family, including a stack of American comics for Robert and two seven-pound tins of lamb's tongue for his wife. For a brief time the whole family was together, apart from Mary's husband, Maurice, who had been transferred to an army camp in Scotland.

But Mrs Wickens began to long for London again. One day, while she was visiting a friend down south, the woman mentioned she would soon be moving away from the East End.

'Has anybody spoken for your place?' Mrs Wickens asked. 'Do you think you could put in a word for us?'

Three months later, Robert and his family were on the move again, this time to a house in Whitwell Road, Plaistow, a couple of miles from their old flat in Poplar. It was one of the few Victorian properties in the neighbourhood that had survived the Blitz unscathed. The local church had been wiped out altogether, and much of the old housing stock with it.

Robert had to get used to a new house in a new area, but at least all the furniture was familiar. Mrs Wickens had arranged for Pickfords to move their belongings out of the storage depot where they had been sitting since the block of flats was bombed. Robert hadn't seen their old kitchen table for years, and he had almost forgotten that they owned a wind-up record player. He felt reassured being surrounded by their old things again.

Robert started at yet another school and gradually got used to life in Plaistow. But more change was just around the corner. When Maurice was stationed down south again, Mary announced she would be moving out. She had managed to get a council flat in Romford for herself, Maurice and little Barbara.

Mary leaving meant Robert would get a bedroom of his own, rather than having to share with Barbara. But even so, he felt very sad to see them go. Despite the huge age gap between him and Mary, they had always been incredibly close, while Barbara had come to feel like a sibling to him.

As he waved them goodbye, Robert was still blissfully unaware of the truth: that the woman now leaving to start a life with her new family was not actually his elder sister, but his mum.

Robert never knew whether Mary told Maurice the truth about him. It wasn't until several years later, long after the war was over, that he himself learned the full story of where he had come from. One day, he was looking through some documents in a drawer in Mrs Wickens's bedroom when he came across a 'penny policy' taken out in his name at birth. These cheap life insurance policies were common among poor families, intended to cover the cost of burying a child at a time when infant mortality rates were high. When Robert looked at the box on the form marked 'Father', he found written there not Mr Wickens but Mr Wilson – the name of Mary's father, Mrs Wickens's first husband. Robert knew that Mr Wilson had been dead long before he himself was born and couldn't possibly be his father.

Then the penny dropped: Robert was illegitimate, and Mary was his mother.

Many years later, a DNA test identified Robert's father as an American sailor by the name of Green. While his ship was moored in the London docks, he had enjoyed a brief fling with Mary, and never came back to discover what he had left behind.

Robert never let on to Mary or Mrs Wickens that he had discovered his true parentage. His mother and grand-mother thought they had shielded him from the truth, and he wasn't going to be the one to tell them otherwise.

Both women were approaching a hundred when they eventually passed away. They died believing that they had carried the secret to their graves.

4

BRIAN

It wasn't only London that was blitzed by the Luftwaffe. In the latter half of 1940, the Germans began launching intensive bombing campaigns against other industrial cities too, particularly in the Midlands. Birmingham, a major producer of munitions, aircraft and vehicles for the war effort, was an obvious target. The city's Rover, Austin and GEC plants were now busy making Hurricanes, Stirlings and Lancasters for the RAF, while other companies had set up new 'shadow factories' to produce aircraft in addition to their regular output, such as Morris Motors' 345-acre site at Castle Bromwich.

Brian Ingram's father worked at the Castle Bromwich plant making Spitfires, while his mother served in the canteen of the Holder and Bishop factory, which was now manufacturing aeroplane and gun parts. Brian had been only one year old when war broke out, and he couldn't remember a time before it. To him, blackouts, rationing and air-raid shelters were just part of everyday life.

The Ingrams lived at Number 10, Upper Cox Street, in Balsall Heath, just south of Birmingham city centre. Theirs was a typical two-up, two-down Victorian terraced house, with an outdoor loo and a tin bath for washing in once a week. Mrs Ingram insisted on keeping the front parlour with the piano in it for 'best', so the family spent virtually all their time in the back room, where there was a big chair by the coal fire for Dad and a smaller one for Mum. The dresser where Mrs Ingram had previously displayed her best plates was now empty, since she had hidden all her ornaments away in a box under the stairs in case of air raids.

Mrs Ingram wasn't one to take risks. She had lost her first child, a little girl, at just two weeks old. Her second, Malcolm, was four when war broke out and had been immediately evacuated to rural Leicestershire. Mal was incensed that baby Brian had been allowed to stay at home while he was exiled to the countryside, and as time passed, his resentment about this perceived injustice only grew.

The Ingrams did their best to visit Mal as often as possible. Mr Ingram took little Brian to see his brother every other Sunday, making the sixty-mile round trip on his only day off, after putting in a fifty-hour week at the factory. On the way back, he often had to walk the four miles to the train station with Brian on his shoulders, since the buses were so infrequent. The routine was beginning to take its toll on poor Mr Ingram, especially since he also volunteered three nights a week as an air-raid warden.

Brian's father loved his voluntary work and often took his son to visit his ARP post, one of 450 now dotted around the city. It was in an empty shop on the high street and had a room at the back with a snooker table in it, where the men whiled away many a happy hour in the early months of the war.

On top of the day job and his voluntary ARP work, Mr Ingram still found time for his true passion in life: performing. He was a skilled ventriloquist, magician, singer and comedian. He made all his ventriloquist dummies himself out of papier mâché and had even given one of them a dark-blue ARP uniform to match his own, complete with a little whistle.

Mr Ingram had always been much in demand at children's parties, but the war had brought him new opportunities to showcase his talents. He had been called on to entertain the ARP, the St John Ambulance and the fire service, among others, helping boost morale with his trademark Brummie humour. He would practise his act at home, where little Brian always provided a captive audience, but the young lad was never allowed to attend the public shows since he was apt to shout out all the secrets to the magic tricks.

Brian's uncles were all doing their bit for the war effort too. Mr Ingram's brother, George, was a fellow ARP warden, while on his wife's side of the family, Uncle Bernard had volunteered for the army and Uncle Horace had joined the Home Guard – the so-called 'dad's army' set up to defend the nation in the event of invasion. Uncle Horace had been issued with a rifle that sadly didn't come with any bullets, but it did make a loud popping sound when he pulled the trigger. 'I don't expect I'll kill many

Germans with it,' he told Brian, 'but I suppose I might frighten one or two of them to death.'

Birmingham's first sighting of the enemy came on 9 August 1940, when a lone pilot flew over and bombed the suburb of Erdington. The Fry family, who lived on Montague Road, lost their house in the raid and were buried under the rubble. Neighbours and ARP workers quickly dug out Mr and Mrs Fry and their daughters, but it took two hours to retrieve their eighteen-year-old son, Jimmy, who was home on leave from the army. Jimmy was rushed to hospital but died on the way there – the first Brummie to be killed by a German bomb.

Regular small raids continued throughout August, September and October. Brian, by now two and a half, got used to being plucked from his warm bed at night and taken out through the cold back yard to the Anderson shelter. As they went, he would see the family next door heading into their own shelter, the wife and daughters leading the husband, who had been blinded by mustard gas in the last war.

Once they were safely inside the shelter, Brian's mother would lay him down to sleep on an old bedframe, but since it was too damp to keep a mattress down there, the metal springs always dug into his back. At least his dad had installed an electric light and a heater, so the shelter would gradually begin to warm up.

Little Brian was familiar with the characteristic *wom-wom-wom* sound the German planes made, and didn't feel afraid in the shelter. He would soon drift off to sleep, while his mother's knitting needles clicked frantically throughout the raids.

Every now and then, his father would pop back from the ARP post to check on the two of them and bring updates on what was happening outside. One night, news came that the aircraft factory in Castle Bromwich where Mr Ingram worked had been bombed, killing five workers. Another night, the Birmingham Small Arms (BSA) factory where Uncle Horace worked was hit. By the end of September, more than a hundred Brummies had lost their lives in the raids, and hundreds more had been injured.

During a brief lull in early October, Winston Churchill's wife, Clementine, visited the city, touring factories and neighbourhoods affected by the bombing. She spoke to one couple who had lost their home but whose defiant attitude reflected that of most Brummies at the time. 'Our house is down,' they told her, 'but our spirits are still up!'

The Luftwaffe returned in force that night, and on the nights that followed. The Empire Theatre was gutted by fire, and the Hippodrome only escaped the same fate thanks to a few brave staff members who managed to smother the incendiary bombs that landed on its roof.

On 25 October, during one of the heaviest raids, a bomb exploded in the orchestra pit of the Carlton cinema in Sparkbrook, only a mile away from the Ingrams' house. It was just after eight in the evening, and the adventure film *Typhoon* starring Dorothy Lamour and Robert Preston was showing. Most of those watching it were teenagers.

Those sitting in the stalls beneath the balcony had some protection from the blast, but the people in the rows closest to the screen were not so lucky. They were found with their eyes wide open, as if still watching the film, but all of them were dead.

Fifteen-year-old Ted Byrne had been talked into going to the Carlton by his friends, despite having already seen the movie. A couple of hours later, his father was among the members of the Home Guard who helped carry the bodies out of the cinema. Ted was pulled from the wreckage alive and taken to Selly Oak Hospital, where his dad went to see him as soon as he could. A nurse brought Mr Byrne to his son's bedside, and he asked Ted if he was all right. Ted opened his eyes and replied, 'Yes, Dad.' Then he closed them again, and passed away. He was one of nineteen people who lost their lives in the tragedy.

Elsewhere in the city that night, another forty people were killed, as the Luftwaffe targeted Birmingham in earnest. Lying on the bedframe in the family's Anderson shelter, little Brian heard the *wom-wom-wom* of the German planes overhead and the crash and bang of bombs nearby.

Mr Ingram came running over from his ARP post and popped his head in at the door of the shelter. 'Balsall Heath Road's all gone,' he told his wife breathlessly. 'And the school's on fire too.'

Brian knew that Mary Street School was where his brother, Mal, had gone before being evacuated, and its playground was just across the road from their house. With the fire services busy trying to save the local factories, the old Victorian building was simply being left to burn. Dad disappeared again, and Mrs Ingram returned to her knitting to calm her nerves.

Later that night, a particularly loud explosion somewhere nearby seemed to lift the Anderson shelter a few inches in the air, before dropping it back into place again. Little Brian soon drifted back to sleep, while his mother's knitting needles clicked even faster than ever.

The next thing Brian knew, it was morning and his mother was wrapping him up in a blanket and carrying him out of the shelter to survey the damage to their home. The loud explosion they had heard in the night turned out to be a parachute mine that had landed next to the Holder and Bishop factory where Mum worked, a few minutes' walk away. The force of the blast had been enough to blow the roof off the Ingrams' house on Upper Cox Street, as well as shattering all of its windows. More alarmingly, the front wall was now bulging outwards, leaving a gap between the bricks and the floorboards. All the ceilings had caved in, and Mrs Ingram's beloved front parlour, which she had always kept so neat and tidy, was showered with plaster dust, while her piano lay face down on the floor.

After salvaging as much as they could, the Ingrams went to stay with Brian's maternal grandparents, who lived half a mile away on St Paul's Road. It would be several months before they were able to return to their home, after the roof had been rebuilt using tiles salvaged from other bombed-out houses and new windows put in under the war damage to property scheme.

The following night the bombers returned, causing further tragedy. Kent Street Public Baths, which was being used as an air-raid shelter, was hit, and a sixty-three-year-old man was killed. A further fifteen people died when a public air-raid shelter in Summer Hill was bombed.

From that day on, the air-raid siren went off every single night for three weeks. Among the buildings damaged were Birmingham's town hall, university, art gallery and cathedral, although luckily Sir Edward Burne-Jones's stained-glass windows had already been removed and put into storage.

Despite the havoc being wreaked on the city, newspaper reports on the bombing didn't mention Birmingham by name, instead referring to it vaguely as 'a Midlands town'. This censorship was intended to avoid handing the enemy any useful information about air-raid damage, but it soon became a source of resentment amongst Brummies.

Brian's father found he got more information about what was happening locally by listening to the propaganda broadcasts put out by Nazi stooge 'Lord Haw-Haw', otherwise known as the Irish fascist William Joyce. It wasn't that Mr Ingram had any sympathy with Haw-Haw's politics, but he was the only person who seemed interested in reporting on what was actually happening in Birmingham, and his programme frequently made reference to the targets of particular local raids, such as the Carlton Cinema.

As little Brian sat playing on the rug by the wireless set, he got used to hearing the programme's opening refrain,

'Germany calling, Germany calling,' delivered in Haw-Haw's affected upper-class English accent, and would prick up his ears whenever he heard places he knew mentioned. It was from Lord Haw-Haw that he and his father first heard that the local King's Heath Public Baths, which were being used as a first-aid post, had been hit at the end of October. Sinister as it was that the German puppet could name the damage to their local area in precise detail, it was at least nice to hear it acknowledged.

As the nights drew in, the Birmingham Blitz only intensified. On 19 November, the city experienced its heaviest bombardment yet, with a raid that lasted nine hours. Numerous factories were damaged, including Fisher and Ludlow, ICI, Lucas Industries, GEC Works and the BSA.

Brian's Uncle Horace was on the night shift at the BSA that evening, working in the New Building where Browning machine guns and Lee Enfield rifles were manufactured. When the siren went at 7.15 p.m., he and his colleagues made their way down to the basement, as planes began to circle overhead and ack-ack guns could be heard in the distance.

Horace and the other workers sat on wooden benches along the sides of the long room, which was lit only by hurricane lamps, chatting about whether the raid that night would be a long one. In the corner, someone began to play the accordion, and soon an impromptu singalong had started.

Outside, showers of incendiary bombs were falling on the factory, but all of them were smothered by fire watchers before they could take hold. Then, just before 9.30 p.m., the workers saw a bright flash and heard a loud thud. It was followed by a terrible crunching sound, as if the floors above them were being crushed by a giant hand. In fact, two bombs had hit the New Building, and it was collapsing storey by storey, bringing hundreds of tons of machinery crashing down upon the poor souls in the basement.

Many of the workers were crushed to death instantly, while others lay injured and dying, trapped beneath fallen concrete, brickwork, machinery and twisted steel girders. Uncle Horace and a colleague were trapped under two pieces of wall that had fallen against each other, protecting them from the debris that rained down from above. All around them lay the dead bodies of their fellow workers who hadn't been so lucky.

Brian's father and Uncle George were among the ARP men who attended the scene that night, along with fire-fighters, Home Guard, rescue teams and first-aid workers. When they arrived, they heard faint cries for help coming from beneath the mountain of rubble. Soon the sound was joined by a horrible crackling noise, as fires caused by the smashed hurricane lamps began to spread, setting off ammunition that was strewn throughout the wreckage.

An emergency SOS was sent to the Birmingham fire service controller, and by 10.30 p.m. more than sixty extra pumps had arrived, many diverted from fires at other factories. As jets of water doused the burning rubble, teams searched for a way to reach the workers trapped inside. The Home Guard managed to rescue five men and a woman by using a rifle as a crowbar to prise open a hole in the fallen debris. The last to get out was an elderly man who escaped just in time, before a mass of debris collapsed and filled in the hole again.

Elsewhere, other rescue workers tunnelled down wherever cries for help could be heard, cutting through steel and masonry. ARP men formed a human conveyor belt to pass the waste material out. After digging one hole of more than five feet, it took a further four hours to free a man and a woman from beneath a wooden bench that had been pinned down at each end by fallen girders. Having sawed the bench in two, the rescue team managed to attach a rope to one half of it and pull, tug-of-war style, until the prisoners were finally freed.

All through the night, rescue workers probed the debris, hoping to find more survivors, but as time went on that was looking increasingly unlikely. Uncle Horace and his colleague were still trapped beneath their two collapsed walls, alive but entombed alongside the corpses of their fellow workers. Water dripped down from the firefighters' hoses above them, and the two men could hear rescue workers digging somewhere close by. But after nearly nine hours, they were too weak to shout for help any more.

Unbeknownst to Horace, Uncle George was part of the rescue team that was operating just a few feet above his head. When the order was given to stop digging, it was George who begged the other men to keep going.

Reluctantly, the exhausted team dug a little bit deeper, just enough to reach Uncle Horace and his colleague. The two men were finally freed from their tomb and brought back up to the world of the living.

A shaken Horace thanked George for saving his life, as he was taken off to the factory surgery on a stretcher to be treated for dehydration and exhaustion.

For the next six weeks, staff at the surgery worked with the demolition squads, identifying bodies that were recovered as the mountain of debris was gradually cleared.

In all, fifty-three workers died that night. If it hadn't been for Uncle George, Horace and his colleague would have made it fifty-five.

Three nights later, the Luftwaffe returned to Birmingham, bombing the BSA yet again, as well as sparking more than 600 separate fires. By the end of the eleven-hour raid, Birmingham was left with just a fifth of its usual water supply. Experts predicted that if another raid came the following evening, fire crews would be unable to save the city.

Thankfully, by the time the bombers did come back, on 3 December, the water mains had been patched up and the fire services were ready to face them once more.

Just over a week later, on 11 December, Birmingham suffered its longest raid of the war, with 200 bombers pummelling the city for more than 13 hours, killing 263 people and seriously injuring 245. The historic St Thomas's Church on Bath Row received a direct hit, its old beams snapping like matchsticks and the pipes of the church organ twisting into mangled shapes, while tombstones were scattered all over the churchyard.

As usual, Brian spent the night in the Anderson shelter with his mother, while his father was out on ARP duty. The following morning, they emerged from the shelter and went back into the house. Mrs Ingram started preparing breakfast as they waited for his father to return.

But there was no sign of Mr Ingram, and in the end they were forced to sit down to eat without him. After they had finished, Mrs Ingram once again took out her knitting, the needles moving more and more quickly as the minutes ticked by.

Then suddenly she leapt out of her chair. 'I'm going out to find Dad,' she told Brian. 'You can play at the neighbours' for a bit.'

After dropping her son off, Mrs Ingram hurried over to the local ARP post. There, she learned that her husband had been badly injured in the raid and taken away in an ambulance. Unfortunately, his colleagues didn't know which hospital he had gone to.

With the city in chaos after the previous night's raid, it took Mrs Ingram several hours to make her way from one hospital to another, searching desperately for her husband. She had no idea what state she would find him in or whether his injuries were life-threatening.

At last, she located him at the Queen Elizabeth Hospital in Bath Row, lying in a bed with bandages wrapped around his head. Mr Ingram, it transpired, had been quite the hero that night. Seeing a little girl trying to put out an incendiary bomb in the street with a bucket of sand, he had recalled a recent warning he and his fellow ARP wardens had been given about the Germans putting delayed-action explosives inside incendiaries. He had run over to the little girl and pushed her out of the way just in time, before the bomb exploded.

Fortunately, Mr Ingram's ARP uniform had protected his body from the blast, but his hands and face were badly burned, and his eyelids were now painfully swollen. It was more than a week before he could return home from hospital, and when he did, his face was still red and puffy. Brian watched him wince as he attempted to shave for the first time.

As far as his wife and son were concerned, Mr Ingram was nothing short of a hero, but he never received any official recognition for his actions – or even a thank you from the family of the girl whose life he had saved.

After a three-month lull, the Luftwaffe returned in force at Easter 1941. Once again, the city's water supply was in a parlous state, and the fire service had to resort to using water that had collected in old bomb craters. The church of St Martin in the Bull Ring was badly damaged, and a high-explosive bomb destroyed many of the graves. The Prince of Wales Theatre on Broad Street was gutted by fire, while the General Hospital was severely damaged and bloodied casualties were sent to the basement of Lewis's department store. Sporadic raids continued until early July, then paused, as the Luftwaffe turned its attention to the Soviet Union.

By now, Mrs Ingram was concerned at how exhausted her husband was getting, juggling his job at the Spitfire factory with his ARP duties and the fortnightly trips to see Brian's brother, Mal, in the countryside. To ease his burden, she decided to bring Mal home. 'If we're going to die, we'd best be all together anyway,' she reasoned.

Although Brian had often visited Mal, at just three years old he was too young to remember a time when his brother had actually lived with him. When Mal arrived at the house on Upper Cox Street, clutching his little suitcase, it felt almost like having a cuckoo in the nest.

For his part, Mal still harboured resentment about having been evacuated while Brian had been allowed to stay at home. He took it out on his little brother frequently, pushing him into a pond, shoving him into a bed of stinging nettles and picking fights with him all the time.

When Mrs Ingram had lost her baby daughter years earlier, she had also lost her faith in God. But now, with two boys at home fighting all day long, she discovered that Sunday School could be a blessing. Brian and Mal were packed off to church every week, so that their mother could get a much-needed break from them.

Brian, meanwhile, was discovering the benefits of having an older brother around, even one who was a bit of a bully. With Mal to keep an eye on him, he was allowed far more freedom than he'd ever had before. The two boys spent many happy afternoons at Cannon Hill Park, where they climbed trees, caught frogs and fished for tiddlers in the bomb craters that had now turned into ponds. If they got thirsty, they snuck into a bombed-out house at the bottom of Cannon Hill Road that still had a working tap and helped themselves to a drink of water.

Other bombed-out houses served as the boys' adventure playgrounds. They climbed wobbly staircases and jumped from beam to beam in upstairs rooms that no longer had any floorboards. Anything they found inside the houses that hadn't already been destroyed by the bombs they happily finished off themselves, smashing windows with gusto and throwing stones at cornices to make chunks of chalk fall down, which they used to draw hopscotch squares on the pavement.

The boys' favourite activity was going out to collect souvenirs after air raids, from still-warm shrapnel to pieces of empty bomb casings, which they proudly brought home to show their horrified mother. On the road opposite Calthorpe Park, where a factory had recently been destroyed, they found lots of different coloured shards of glass, which they immediately added to their collection. Soon, Brian had a whole shoebox full of treasures.

After a bedspring factory at the bottom of Sherbourne Road was hit, the boys found that if they put their arms through the broken windows they could reach the piles of V-shaped springs inside, which made fantastic catapults. A bombed-out hairpin maker's provided the perfect ammunition. The lead from telephone wires in bombed-out shops, meanwhile, could be melted down on the stove and poured into moulds to make toy soldiers.

The makeshift toys were all well and good, but one afternoon the boys were in Calthorpe Park when they came across a much more significant find. Brian was crawling through some bushes in search of shrapnel when he chanced upon a damaged German machine gun, which had evidently fallen from a plane.

It weighed more than he did, and getting it home was a challenge. In the end, he and Malcolm tied the gun to a tree branch using their shoelaces, threw one of their coats over the top to conceal it, and then carried it back between them, like a pair of stretcher-bearers with an injured soldier.

Mrs Ingram was not best pleased when she saw what her sons had brought home. 'Didn't I tell you not to bring any more of that stuff back?' she shouted, apparently oblivious to the boys' excitement.

Their father merely raised an amused eyebrow, secretly rather impressed they had managed to get the gun all the way home without being stopped by the authorities. Even so, it didn't seem right for an ARP warden to be hoarding German armaments, so the next morning he sold it to the local rag-and-bone man.

Mrs Ingram was right to worry about the boys' collecting habit, since some souvenirs were not as harmless as they at first appeared. A chilling film produced by the Ministry of Information warned of the dangers of so-called 'butterfly bombs', tiny 2 kg explosives that would float gently down to earth without exploding – only to detonate later when they were picked up by inquisitive children. The film showed a young boy finding one of the new bombs in his back yard and cheerfully calling out to his mother, 'Look what I've found!' – before he disappeared in a cloud of white smoke.

The message certainly wasn't lost on Mrs Ingram. 'Whatever you do, don't go looking for those butterflies,' she warned her sons, who of course went straight out to Calthorpe Park in search of the thrilling new devices. After several hours, they were disappointed to come back empty-handed.

In the summer of 1942, the Luftwaffe resumed its raids intermittently. On 27 July, there was a morning raid on Solihull, followed by one in Birmingham that evening, with sixty planes raiding the city and causing 283 fires. The Gabriel and Company works, which was manufacturing gun mountings, tank track links and other equipment for the navy, was hit by a high-explosive bomb. Brian's gran and grandad, who had taken the family in while their house was being repaired, were now bombed out themselves and had to move into a small flat in nearby King's Heath.

The last significant raid on Birmingham took place three nights later, killing a dozen people. The following April, a lone pilot dropped his bombs on Little Bromwich, causing injuries but no fatalities. It was the last the Brummies saw of the German bombers.

Throughout the Birmingham Blitz, there had been 65 separate attacks on the city, involving over 5,000 high-explosive bombs, 48 parachute mines, many thousands of incendiaries and a number of oil and phosphorus bombs. In all, 2,000 tons of bombs had been dropped on Birmingham and nearly 5,000 fires reported. Over 12,000 houses were ruined, as were 302 factories.

The air raids had killed 2,241 Brummies, including 211 children under 16 and 77 volunteer ARP wardens.

Yet for Brian, who couldn't remember a time before the Blitz, it had not been a terrible or even a particularly remarkable experience. If anything, he felt a sort of sadness as the bombing raids came to an end. Now there would be no new souvenirs to be scavenged from the rubble, and no newly bombed-out houses to explore.

The greatest source of excitement in his young life was gone, and he couldn't understand why everyone was so happy about it.

5

DOROTHY

Like Brian, six-year-old Dorothy Kedwards was the child of a volunteer ARP warden. Dorothy lived in Sparkbrook – less than a mile away from Brian's home in Balsall Heath. The Carlton Cinema, tragically bombed during the screening of *Typhoon*, was her local picture house, where she and the other kids in the neighbourhood would flock every Saturday morning to watch the latest Popeye cartoons.

But when the German bombers first came to Birmingham, Dorothy was thirty miles away, staying with her Aunt Winnie in Worcester. Her parents had decided that their only child would be safer there than remaining at home with the two of them, since their back yard was so small they didn't even have an Anderson shelter.

The reason for this lay a century earlier, when the city had expanded at a dizzying pace during the Industrial Revolution. The family home, Number 4, back of 63 Larches Street, was – as its address suggested – what was known as a 'back-to-back'. Tens of thousands of these simple homes had been constructed to house the city's growing workforce, sandwiched in between existing properties with regular street addresses. The Kedwardses' tiny cottage was one of six built in a little clump at the end of an alleyway between two of the red-brick terraced houses on Larches Street.

Compared to many of these notorious slum dwellings, which had long since been deemed illegal by the city's planners, the Kedwardses' house was relatively comfortable. It was certainly cramped, but Dorothy had her own bedroom upstairs – large enough, just about, to fit a small wardrobe as well as a bed – while downstairs, a single space served as living and dining room, with a scullery out the back. In the tiny yard, Dorothy's dad had managed to plant a few peas.

Even as a child, Dorothy couldn't help noticing the contrast between her parents' little home and Aunt Winnie's much larger house in Worcester, which overlooked the Lea & Perrins sauce factory – a convenient landmark if she ever got lost, since its vinegary smell could be picked up a mile away.

Aunt Winnie had been a dresser to the stars at one of Birmingham's major theatres, and now lived with her husband, Harold, in a spacious semi-detached villa on Stanley Road. It was one of the largest properties on the street, meaning they had room not just for Dorothy but for a pair of evacuees from Coventry as well.

Dorothy knew she was lucky to be staying with family when other evacuees were living among strangers. But even so, she found it hard to adjust to life in Worcester. She was horrified by the rabbit carcasses her uncle hung up by their feet in the understairs cloakroom, a bucket left underneath to catch the maggots so that he could use them when he went fishing in the River Severn. And while Aunt Winnie was always perfectly nice, she wasn't much of a surrogate parent. She tended to leave the children to their own devices, lying in bed late into the morning rather than getting up when they did. Dorothy struggled to make breakfast and get herself ready in time for school, and frequently got the cane for being late.

Perhaps it was because Aunt Winnie had no children of her own, having lost three babies some years earlier, but Dorothy always felt there was a distance between herself and her aunt. In some ways it reminded her of the relationship she had with her mum, who was also lacking when it came to maternal affection. Dorothy's grandmother hadn't been a great role model to her daughters, turning to drink when their father died and often disappearing from the family home for days at a time, before eventually succumbing to liver failure. As the eldest daughter, Dorothy's mother had been left to bring up her younger siblings herself, a role she hadn't chosen and that didn't come naturally to her.

Dorothy's father, on the other hand, was very different. Mr Kedwards was a naturally warm and affectionate man, and his only child adored him. Dorothy felt lonely at times, and often longed for a little brother or sister, but her father's love was enough to fill the void.

At Aunt Winnie's, Dorothy missed her father terribly but at least the two evacuees from Coventry, Billy and

Ronnie, were friendly, and the neighbour's daughters often invited her round to play. Even with other children around, though, she spent much of her time alone in her bedroom in the attic. She had built a doll's house out of cardboard and made a family of Plasticine figures to go with it, whiling away the hours moving them from room to room and imagining their happy life together.

Her own family, meanwhile, were never far from her thoughts, especially in the autumn of 1940, when the bombs began to rain down on Birmingham. From her attic window, Dorothy could see the telltale red glow in the distance as the city was set alight by the Luftwaffe, and she was filled with worry for her parents.

They too, it seemed, had begun to struggle with being separated from their daughter. Against the advice of the city authorities, they decided to bring Dorothy back home. As Mrs Kedwards explained, in the typically matter-of-fact words used by so many parents at the time, 'If we go, we can all go together.'

Dorothy was thrilled to come home, but thanks to her father's ARP duties she spent most of the air raids with her mother. The two of them soon settled into a regular evening routine. Dorothy would come home from school, eat her tea, have a quick wash and then change into her 'siren suit' – an all-in-one outfit with a hood, designed to keep children warm, and somewhat protected, during long nights in the shelters.

The family cat, who was known as Puss since no one had ever bothered to name him, always seemed to know when the bombers were on their way. Before the siren had even sounded, he would race to the coalhole under the stairs. Dorothy and her mother, meanwhile, would head to the cellar of the local grocery shop.

Parnell's was just a few doors down from them on Larches Street and was owned by the grandmother of one of Dorothy's friends. The underground space was dark and clammy, but the shop had no shortage of candles, and the grown-ups had even dragged a couple of camp beds down there for the children to sleep on during longer raids.

But even with the early warning system provided by their anxious moggy, Dorothy and her mum had to be quick to get down to Parnell's cellar before the bombers arrived. During one raid, they didn't make it inside until the action had already started. Dorothy, who was normally safely sheltered underground when the bombs began to fall, got a glimpse of the terrifying world that her father inhabited at surface level during his shifts with the ARP. As bombs whistled and crashed nearby, she was hit on the head by a burning piece of shrapnel, which scorched the hood of her siren suit and then dropped to the ground, still smouldering. From then on, Mrs Kedwards made sure to get her daughter to the shelter as soon as she saw the cat dashing under the stairs.

But as the nights of the Blitz gave way to weeks, and the weeks to months, a mixture of exhaustion and complacency crept in. One evening, when the cat ran for cover and the siren began to wail, Mrs Kedwards decided she wasn't budging. 'Oh sod it,' she said. 'We're staying here tonight!'

Dorothy knew her dad wouldn't approve, but she could see the exhaustion on her mother's face and she didn't dare to contradict her. It was a cold night, so the two of them snuggled up in bed together while they waited for the all clear to sound.

In the event, the raid wasn't a particularly bad one and their little house remained in one piece. But as Dorothy had predicted, Mr Kedwards was furious when he found out his wife and daughter hadn't taken shelter. Dorothy had never seen him look so angry – not even when the Luftwaffe had dropped an incendiary on their tiny back yard and torched his precious row of peas. After that, she and her mother always went straight to the shelter.

It was just as well, since the raids were beginning to hot up. Even down in the Parnell's cellar, Dorothy could tell the number of bombs falling each night was increasing. Sat in the candlelit underground room, she could hear the thuds and crumps as they exploded overhead. But more ominous still was the noise of the German planes' engines as they flew over. There was something about that heavy, uneven drone that chilled her even more than the sound of the bombs.

One night, the drone of the planes was louder than ever, and so too, Dorothy thought, were the explosions. The bombs were falling closer to home than usual, and with each one the whole cellar seemed to vibrate. Then came the loudest of all – a mine, which exploded in the middle of Larches Street, ripping through a water main and shattering eight houses in one fell swoop.

The next morning, Dorothy and her mother stared at the damage wrought by the mine. There was a massive hole in the middle of the road, and the houses had been hollowed out by the explosion, leaving only empty shells. Looking up at one of the shattered windows, Dorothy saw a dog that had been killed while trying to escape, its lifeless body draped over the sill. She had always loved animals, and the sight of the poor creature affected her deeply.

Fortunately, her own cat, Puss, had made it through the raid unscathed. But for the time being at least, the Parnell's cellar had been rendered out of bounds. The burst pipe was disgorging water into the street and before long the cellar had flooded. That night, Dorothy and her mum sought refuge in their entryway instead – the little covered passageway between the houses on Larches Street that led down to their cluster of back-to-backs.

It was, in fact, more sturdy than it looked. Dorothy had noticed, while exploring the bomb-wrecked houses of the neighbourhood in the daytime, that the arched roofs of the entries often survived when the buildings around them had crumbled. But up at street level, the noise of the German planes was louder than ever, and every explosion sent a blast of warm air down the narrow passageway. She and her mother had dragged a mattress and eiderdown into the entry, in the vain hope of catching some sleep that night, but while the arched brickwork offered some protection from flak and shrapnel, the two of them felt more exposed than ever. Dorothy was very relieved, a few days later, to learn that the Parnell's cellar had been successfully dried out and could be used as a shelter once again.

Meanwhile, other local buildings were beginning to sustain more serious damage and the landscape around Dorothy's home was changing. With whole houses wiped off the map, it was now possible to see all the way from Larches Street through to the road that ran parallel to it, Long Street. But more shocking still was when her school on Stratford Road sustained a direct hit, rendering much of the building unsuitable for teaching.

Dorothy and her classmates were shuffled around several local abandoned houses, sitting cross-legged on the floor of the empty front rooms while the teachers tried their best to deliver their lessons. The kids were under strict instructions not to go upstairs, in case of any as-yet-unnoticed bomb damage that might make the buildings unsafe.

The teachers, not to mention the parents, would have been horrified to know that the kids were already treating the bombed-out houses further down the road as their playgrounds. Dorothy and her friends had found their way into the cellar of one of the ruined properties and she loved nothing better than sneaking down there with a couple of her mum's candles to play 'house'.

Dorothy was good at using her imagination, since her parents never had much money for toys. Her father had an artistic streak, however, and had taught himself to make a few popular ones: wooden parrots that swung back and forth on their perches, and clowns that moved when you pressed the base they stood on.

They weren't just for Dorothy's benefit either. With Christmas approaching, the local shops were desperate for stock and many of them were more than happy to buy Mr Kedwards's homemade wares.

Soon, Dorothy had become her father's unofficial apprentice and the two of them had their own cottage industry, working away like Santa's elves every weekend churning out the simple wooden toys. With the help of a guide she found in a bookshop in town, she mastered the art of making crepe paper flowers, and before long her roses, gladioli and sweet peas were on sale in the local stores too.

At school, Dorothy's artistic flair was soon noticed. One day, she showed her teachers a drawing she had done of a baby in a cot, copied from a picture that hung above the fireplace in her parents' bedroom.

'Did you draw this?' her teacher asked in astonishment.

'Yes, Miss,' she replied.

The teacher was so impressed that she set Dorothy up with a paper and pencils then and there, while the rest of the class went on with their regular work.

If there was one thing Dorothy loved more than art it was music, and here it was her mother who encouraged her talents. Mrs Kedwards's prized possession was an old upright piano, which she had taught herself to play by ear. When Dorothy began showing an interest in the instrument, she was determined she should learn to play it properly, so she arranged for her to have lessons with an elderly lady called Miss Edwards.

Dorothy always seemed to arrive just as the teacher was finishing her tea. The old woman would open the door and then delicately place a tea towel over her plate, hiding the remnants of her boiled egg and soldiers. Only then would they get down to the serious business of music.

Before long, Dorothy was travelling into town to take her piano exams, which were conducted at the Imperial Hotel. She passed each one with distinction, but with every level the cost of the exam got higher, and eventually she reached a point where her parents couldn't afford to pay for them any more.

Music had become Dorothy's passion, and she loved to tune in to the BBC's Home Service, delighting in everything from music-hall classics to sweeping orchestral performances. But Mrs Kedwards made sure to supervise her listening, turning off the little Vidor wireless set whenever she heard the bongs introducing the BBC news. 'We can do without that rubbish,' she told her.

The truth was Mrs Kedwards was protecting her daughter, doing her best to shield her from the harsh realities of a world at war. Living through the bombing raids was bad enough. The last thing Dorothy needed was constant updates on military disasters taking place in faraway lands.

But despite Mrs Kedwards's best efforts, she couldn't entirely keep the horrors of war at bay. Dorothy had witnessed a dramatic change in her Uncle Wilf, who had come back from Dunkirk deeply traumatised after seeing one of his comrades decapitated in front of him. Her uncle's friend, Dorothy learned, had kept on running even after his head had been blown off.

Once a chatty, confident young man, Uncle Wilf had returned from the Continent with a stutter that would stay with him for the rest of his life. He now suffered from chronic asthma, and his expectations for the future had been affected too. 'I'll never marry,' he told his sister sadly. 'I wouldn't want to burden anyone with the way I am now.'

For Mrs Kedwards, who had pretty much raised him from childhood, the change in her brother was heart-breaking.

Like many children in wartime, Dorothy's health was somewhat precarious. To combat poor nutrition caused by rationing and food shortages, the government had brought in a scheme whereby poorer children were entitled to free orange juice and cod liver oil. But when the nurse at Dorothy's school examined her, she decided she was still looking a little peaky and referred her to a clinic for 'sunray therapy'. Every week, Dorothy and her mum would walk to the clinic, then Dorothy would strip down to her knickers and put on a pair of dark goggles before lying down on a mat under an ultraviolet lamp.

As medical treatments went, it was pretty inoffensive, even for a nervous young child. But it did nothing to prevent Dorothy from developing a nasty case of whooping cough. When she began suffering from bronchitis as well, she found herself coughing so badly that she felt she was going to pass out.

Fortunately, the local doctor was just around the corner on Stratford Road – a frail old lady who looked like she could do with a few sunray treatments herself. Dr Smith took one look at Dorothy and wasted no time calling an ambulance.

Dorothy was whisked off to Little Bromwich Hospital three miles away, with the bell of the ambulance clanging throughout the journey. There, she was admitted to an isolation ward, where a group of other children were also receiving treatment.

Most of the kids were younger than Dorothy and slept in cots, but since she had a bed, once she was feeling a little better she could get up and explore the ward when the nurses were out of sight. She soon found that her freedom of movement put a target on her back, however. An older boy, who was unable to leave his own bed, began threatening her, demanding that unless she stole the rusks left for the babies and handed them over to him, he would beat her up as soon as he was well enough.

Terrified, Dorothy did as he said, sneaking around the ward and pinching the biscuits from the crying babies to hand over to the greedy bully.

Other than her tormentor, barely anyone spoke to Dorothy on the isolation ward. The nurses who flitted in now and then were concerned purely with the medical welfare of their patients. None of them showed her the slightest bit of warmth or human kindness.

Her parents visited, but they were only allowed to stand at the door of the ward and wave at her through the window. For Dorothy, it was the loneliest few weeks of her life.

Eventually, though, the time came for her to be discharged. This time, Mr and Mrs Kedwards both came to the hospital to collect her. Her dad had taken the day off work and cycled over, while her mum had travelled there on the tram.

On the way home, Dorothy and her mum sat on the back seat of the tram so that they could watch her dad following behind them on his bike. He was a fast cyclist and had no difficulty keeping up, but with his eyes on his wife and daughter, he wasn't paying much attention to the road.

Dorothy watched in horror as her dad's front wheel got stuck in one of the tram rails, flipping the bike over and throwing him on to the ground.

Fortunately, the traffic was light at the time and Mr Kedwards escaped being run over, but he did have a nasty gash down one leg where the pedal of the bike had cut into his skin. While Dorothy and her mum trundled home on the tram, Dad turned around and limped all the way back to the hospital to get it seen to. It was several hours before the family was finally reunited back on Larches Street.

Dorothy had seen enough of the war to know that her family was lucky to all be together. Other kids at her school had lost parents to the German bombs or had fathers and uncles who never returned from the fighting.

But she had never quite shaken the feeling that three was a rather lonely number. Even being back at home with both of her parents it felt as if someone was missing. For as long as she could remember, Dorothy had longed for a sibling, so when she was told that her mother 'had a baby in her tummy', she could not have been more excited.

The timing was perfect. According to the midwife's best estimate, the little boy or girl would arrive on 30 June, the same day that Dorothy had been born. She couldn't have dreamed of a better birthday present.

In the event, baby Angela arrived two days late, much to Dorothy's annoyance. But from the moment she saw her, she was besotted with her baby sister.

Now, at last, Dorothy had the happy family she had always dreamed of.

6

DOREEN

In large, sprawling cities like London and Birmingham, even the most intense bombing raids were relatively spread out. But towards the end of 1940, Luftwaffe commander Hermann Goering had his eye on a different kind of target: a smaller city, ideally with some strategic significance, that could be virtually wiped off the map in a single night. The propaganda value of such a raid, he felt, would be huge.

Goering found the perfect target in Coventry, an industrial city just twenty miles from Birmingham and only a sixth of its size. Boasting factories supplying everything from Merlin aircraft engines to military staff cars, it was integral to the British war effort, and as a medieval walled city, it was also relatively compact.

The planned raid was scheduled for 14 November, when a full moon would provide the best possible visibility. It was codenamed Operation Moonlight Sonata after Beethoven's famous piano piece, but the brutal reality of what happened that night belied the romantic name.

In fact, the raid proved so horrifyingly effective as an example of devastating aerial bombardment that it spawned a new German word, *coventrieren*. An English translation soon followed: 'to coventrate'.

Six-year-old Doreen Johnson, like the rest of her fellow Coventrians, had no idea of the carnage that was coming her way. In the preceding months, the city had suffered a series of relatively modest raids. Seventeen separate sorties had left 176 local people dead and 229 seriously injured.

Doreen had grown used to spending her evenings in the family's Anderson shelter on Adderley Street, along with her mother and her little black-and-white terrier, Jim. The wail of the air-raid siren was enough to induce a raft of reciprocal howling from all the other neighbourhood dogs, but as long as he was with her, Doreen's little companion was always quiet and content. Her mother did her best to make the shelter as cosy as possible, and they snuggled up together in a nest of blankets and pillows. Mrs Johnson always kept a fresh bottle of water in the kitchen, ready to be grabbed as soon as she heard the siren, along with enough food to get them through the night.

Doreen's older brother, Ron, had been evacuated from the city at the start of the war, joining 3,000 local kids who had decamped to the countryside. Mr Johnson believed in letting children make decisions for themselves, and when he had asked her whether she wanted to go too she had been adamant, insisting, 'I want to stay with Mum.' She was only dimly aware of the dangers that awaited her at home, but whatever they were, she felt she would rather be by her mother's side than with strangers.

Mr Johnson himself had grown up with a domineering Victorian father. As a result, he was a quiet, nervous man, who suffered so badly with stress in later years that he developed alopecia. But despite his anxious personality, he had ended up working not one but two demanding jobs to support his family.

By day, he toiled at Brett's stamping works, which supplied machine parts to the Triumph factory in town, where motorbikes were assembled for the army. It was heavy work, and his wife would always do her best to feed him up for it, sending him off in the morning with a large sandwich filled with whatever meat they had in the house, even if it meant she and Doreen went without.

When he was finished at the factory, Mr Johnson would set off into town for a shift at the Hand and Heart pub on Gosford Street. At least, as everybody knew, pubs were among the safest places to be when the German bombers came, since their deep beer cellars made ideal shelters. As much as Mrs Johnson worried about her husband's health, she knew he was probably better protected at work than she and Doreen were in the little Anderson shelter in the back yard.

Despite Mr Johnson working two jobs, the family lived pretty much on the breadline. Doreen had few toys, her clothes were mostly patched-up and secondhand, and as far as she was concerned, taking a bus was tantamount to a holiday. But her parents always did the best they could for her. When another girl at school received a doll's house for her birthday, Doreen complained that she didn't even have a doll. Her father duly found an old one with an arm and a leg missing in the local secondhand shop and gave it to his wife for a bit of reconstructive surgery with her needle and thread. Then he took an old packing crate and cut windows and a door in the front to make a little house for it to live in.

Another time, when one of her school friends teased her for having a hole in her shoe, Doreen rushed home in floods of tears. When Mrs Johnson discovered the reason, she stayed up late into the night repairing the shoe herself, going over it with whitening so that it looked as good as new. The next day, Doreen showed off her shoes to her approving friends, telling them that her mum had just bought them for her.

To Doreen, the greatest treat in life was getting faggots and peas for tea from her favourite pie shop in town, as and when the family could afford it. One wintry November evening, when she was feeling particularly hungry, she begged her mother to take her there.

Mrs Johnson turned her purse out on the table to see if she had enough money. 'I think I can spare *that* much,' she said, pushing a few coins towards her daughter.

It should be enough, Mrs Johnson reckoned, to cover the cost of their tea that evening – including the little morsels that she knew Doreen would share with her beloved dog, Jim.

Mr Garner, who ran the pie shop, was used to customers who were stretching the pennies. He would weigh up whatever they could afford to give him against what he could afford to offer in return. Doreen watched excitedly as he doled out two-and-a-half faggots and three spoonfuls of peas into their bowl. Her mother thanked him, before whipping a tea towel out of her pocket and carefully folding it over the top of the bowl to keep the food warm until they got home.

On their way back, the air-raid siren started wailing. There was no time to make it home and get inside the Anderson shelter, so Mrs Johnson made for the nearest pub, at the top of King William Street, begging the landlord to let them into the cellar. Jim would just have to do without his scraps of faggot this time, she told Doreen. She was sure he'd be perfectly safe under the kitchen table.

By the time the first bombs began falling, a little after 7 p.m., there were two dozen people in the pub cellar. The walls were damp and the air suffused with the musty smell of stale beer, but at least there was a bit of light down there, thanks to a single light bulb hanging from the ceiling. The landlord provided water, and Doreen and her mother shared their faggots and peas with the people crouching next to them.

It was a long night. Nobody down in the cellar knew it at the time, but the raid going on above their heads would turn out to be the most intense of the war so far. Little Doreen cowered, terrified, at the muffled explosions she could hear overhead. Her mother was praying furiously under her breath. 'Heavenly Father, watch over my family and keep them safe . . .'

As the hours passed, with no let-up from the bombs, Doreen began to notice something strange. It had been a cold, frosty evening when she and her mother had dived inside the pub, but as the night wore on, even underground in the dank cellar, she could feel the temperature rising.

Up above them, the city was on fire. Tens of thousands of incendiary bombs had already fallen that night, along with hundreds of tons of high explosives. The Germans were also dropping 250 kg *Flammenbombes*, each containing fifty gallons of petrol. With the city lit up by hundreds of individual fires, the job had got much easier for the next wave of bombers.

Volunteer firefighters all over Coventry were doing their best to tackle the blaze, in circumstances that were apocalyptic. In the city centre, a stream of boiling butter was oozing like lava from the damaged Maypole Dairy. Elsewhere a woman had caught fire and was being bundled to the ground by an ARP warden, who tried desperately to stifle the flames.

All over the city, kids like Doreen were cowering in their shelters. In her dressing room at the New Hippodrome, a five-year-old Julie Andrews was hiding under a table, while a team of stagehands on the roof did their best to stop the theatre from going up in flames.

A few miles away, in the suburb of Hollbrooks, a sixteen-year-old girl was hiding in an understairs cupboard when her house was destroyed by the blast from a bomb. She was blown out into the street by the force, her clothes torn from her body. The poor girl survived the ordeal but the shock of what she had been through left her mute for the best part of a week.

At Gulson Road Hospital, a four-year-old girl was brought in by ambulance. She had no visible wounds but her puffy cheeks offered a clue to what had happened. The blast from a bomb had burst her little lungs, and there was nothing anyone could do to save her.

All night, the relentless bombing raid continued. By midnight, the city's magnificent Gothic cathedral had burned to the ground, leaving only the tower and outer wall still standing. By now it looked less like an active site of worship and more like the ruins of an ancient castle.

All told, the raid lasted eleven hours, the most concentrated period of bombing experienced anywhere in Britain during the war. Fortunately, Doreen slept through most of it, snuggled up in her mother's arms. Despite the thudding explosions overhead, she was used to drifting off during long nights in the family Anderson shelter. By the time the power to the pub cut out, plunging those sheltering in the cellar into darkness, Doreen was already fast asleep.

The following day, she awoke to the sound of the all-clear siren. To Doreen, that long, constant tone always felt like Christmas morning. But the presents the Germans had left for the people of Coventry that night were far from welcome.

When Doreen and her mother emerged from the pub cellar, much of the city was still on fire, and there was smoke billowing all around them. The reddish tint of the sky looked more like an African sunset than a winter's morning in the Midlands.

All around them was devastation and chaos, with lamp-posts bent and twisted over on themselves and tram rails ripped from the ground, reaching upwards towards the red sky. Fountains of water gushed from burst pipes, and sparks of electricity arced from torn power cables.

Vast piles of bricks and rubble lay where only the night before there had been shops and homes. Some had been ripped open like doll's houses, revealing the owners' domestic lives to the world. Others had collapsed altogether. Books, clothes and kitchenware littered the streets. Broken glass crunched underfoot, and torn blackout curtains flapped in the wind.

Worst of all were the human remains. As she walked along the street, Doreen grasped her mother's arm tightly, burying her face in the folds of her warm winter coat. Her mother told her to keep her eyes shut, but even so she caught glimpses of horrors that she would never forget. Some of the corpses were intact, others brutally dismembered. All over the city, arms, legs and even heads were already being gathered up by the authorities. With more than 500 dead and nearly 1,000 more seriously injured, it was a gruesome jigsaw puzzle matching up the body parts for burial.

And it wasn't just humans who had felt the full force of the raid. Those animals that had survived the bombardment were wandering the streets in confusion, barking, howling and mewling as they tried to work out what had happened to their homes and to the people who normally looked after them. Other pets had been even less fortunate. The torn bodies of cats and dogs seemed to be everywhere. One family even found a dead horse lying on their doorstep.

'Can I open my eyes now, Mummy?' Doreen asked anxiously, as her mother led her towards home.

'Not just yet,' Mrs Johnson told her. 'Leave them closed a bit longer.'

They stepped gingerly over rubble and past injured and traumatised people. Even with her eyes closed, Doreen couldn't shut out the sound of their cries and screams, and she could feel the heat of the fires that were still burning all around.

Eventually, she and her mother made it back to Adderley Street. But when she opened her eyes, Doreen couldn't see any sign of their home. A 1,000kg 'Hermann' bomb had landed on it, flattening the house and all its contents.

Doreen spotted her father standing a few feet away, staring blankly at the place where the Anderson shelter had once been.

'Dad!' she shouted.

Mr Johnson turned around and she saw his eyes widen as he caught sight of her. Then he dropped to the ground, unconscious.

'He's fainted,' shouted a nearby policeman, one of a handful of men who had been combing through the rubble. He carried Mr Johnson over to the side of the road and tried to revive him. 'It's all right,' he told Doreen's father. 'Look, your wife and daughter are here now.'

When Mr Johnson came round and saw that what the man said was true, he couldn't believe his eyes. After he had returned from the pub where he had been sheltering all night and found their house obliterated, he had assumed that the rest of the family had gone with it. He could scarcely believe that all three of them had survived the raid intact.

There was one member of the family who hadn't been so lucky, however. The body of Doreen's little dog, Jim, lay somewhere underneath all the rubble, but try as they might, the Johnsons couldn't find it.

Doreen couldn't stop crying as she thought of Jim all alone under the kitchen table, waiting for her and her mum to come home, as bombs went off all around him. The only thing her parents could say to reassure her was that, given the scale of the damage, his death must have been instantaneous.

ARP wardens were already sorting through the rubble, making piles of bricks that could be used to rebuild homes elsewhere. The only thing the Johnsons managed to salvage from the debris of their home was a tiny silver cup, which Doreen had won in a baby contest when she was fourteen months old. She held on to it tightly, as the three of them piled into the back of a police car for the short drive to her grandmother's house in Red Lane, just under a mile away. The little cup was all she had left of the life she had left behind just twelve hours earlier.

As they drove through the bomb-damaged streets, safely ensconced in the back of the police car, Doreen got a better look at what would soon become known as 'the martyred city'.

Coventry had been comprehensively ruined. Some 350 roads were blocked with rubble, 300 gas mains damaged and 1,000 sewers fractured. A third of the city's shops had been either destroyed completely or were so badly damaged that they were unable to carry on trading. At the Council House in the town centre, which had remarkably come through more or less unscathed, a queue of people snaked around the block, waiting to check the list of the dead for the names of their loved ones.

More than 50,000 people had taken to the road, fleeing the city in search of safety further afield. Mothers were pushing heavy prams laden with belongings, their infants sitting on top of the piles.

But even with fires still raging all over the city, people were beginning to come together to help each other rebuild and recover. And it wasn't just the locals – other nearby cities had come to Coventry's aid as well. Forty ambulances had already arrived from outside the city, and 20,000 blankets were on their way by train from London.

Within a week, the Women's Voluntary Service had established seventy pop-up canteens, offering free food to

20,000 people every day, and rationing was temporarily suspended. Everywhere you looked, it seemed people were helping each other, whether it was to eat, stay warm or find a roof to sleep under.

At least Doreen's grandmother's house was undamaged, though she wasn't exactly set up for visitors. Doreen and her parents had to sleep on blankets laid out on the hard living-room floor, with a potty in the corner in case one of them needed the toilet in the night. The little cottage was very basic, with no electricity and, for the moment at least, no drinking water, since the raid had wiped out the city's supply. Government vans were already touring the streets, issuing warnings via loudspeaker that all water should be boiled to prevent a typhoid outbreak.

For the rest of that day, the main thought on most people's minds – those, at least, who hadn't joined the mass evacuation to the surrounding villages – was whether the German bombers would return that evening. Granny's Anderson shelter was much the same as their own – dank, cramped and totally defenceless against a direct hit. But it was better than nothing and at least slightly safer than staying in the house.

In the event, the night passed without incident. For the Germans, this was a huge missed opportunity, perhaps one of the biggest of the war. Goering had hoped that a small city like Coventry could be brought to its knees by a single concentrated raid, and that the level of devastation meted out in the course of one night would be enough to crush the morale of the citizens altogether. But, despite what they had suffered, the people of Coventry dusted themselves down and got on with their lives.

The British government, meanwhile, feared a collapse of law and order. Over the next few days, more than 200 extra policemen were sent to the city to guard against potential riots and looting. Home Secretary Herbert Morrison, and even King George VI, put in appearances, doing their best to boost morale. But the Germans didn't return, and Coventry – just about – held firm.

In the Johnson family, though, the experience had taken its toll. Doreen's father developed an infection in one of his teeth, and when the dentist told him he would have to have it removed, he fainted again, collapsing on the floor of the surgery. In the end, the only way he could get through the procedure was for the dentist to pay him a home visit, ethyl chloride and all.

Even at six years old, Doreen realised that her father's behaviour wasn't quite normal, but she too had been marked by the events of that terrifying night. The experience had caused her to develop a bad case of claus-trophobia. Going into Granny's Anderson shelter became increasingly difficult for her, especially when her mother tried to fit a gas mask over her face.

'Please, Mum, don't put it on me!' Doreen begged, despite Mrs Johnson's protestations that the mask might save her life.

*

The Germans did return to Coventry a second time, in a seven-hour raid just before Easter the following year that claimed the lives of another 281 people. For Doreen and her family, it was an even closer shave than before. While the first big raid had been tightly focused on the city centre, this one was more spread out, and her grandmother's street was right in the firing line.

The whole family had gathered in Granny's Anderson shelter when there was a furious banging on the back gate. 'Get out! Get out!' came the voice of an ARP warden. 'There's a bomb round the back of the shelter that hasn't gone off yet!'

The four of them rushed up the garden path without stopping to look behind them, belting through the house and on to the road. Outside, another bomb had left a gaping crater, which had swallowed a car whole. Doreen could see the driver still sitting behind the wheel, dead.

Mercifully, the bomb behind Granny's shelter didn't go off, and once it had been safely removed by the authorities the Johnsons were able to move back in. But Doreen couldn't shake the feeling that the Germans were out to get them personally. It felt like she and her parents kept cheating death by a whisker.

In the aftermath of the second big raid, the local people once again rallied round each other. Doreen lost count of the number of times a friendly neighbour dropped in to offer a spare bit of bread or a cup of milk. In some badly blitzed streets families who no longer had functioning kitchens would gather around communal campfires, sharing their meagre meals with friends and strangers alike. Despite all the tragedy she had witnessed, seeing how people came together and helped one another made a deep impression on Doreen, one that would stay with her for many years to come.

In September 1940, just before the Blitz on London began, Hitler had warned that the German Air Force would not just bomb British cities but 'erase' them. In Coventry, the Luftwaffe had come their closest to achieving that aim. In the first raid alone, it had dropped 500 tons of high explosives and 30,000 incendiaries, killing an estimated 568 people and destroying or damaging more than 43,000 homes.

But the city survived, and so too did the vast majority of its people. The wreck of the old Gothic cathedral still stands today, a monument to the worst night in Coventry's history. But right next to it towers the magnificent New Cathedral, a bold 1960s edifice that embodies the fierce determination to go on.

7

BETTY

All over the country, aircraft manufacturers had become prime targets for the German bombers. Filton, a small town north of Bristol, was home to the Bristol Aeroplane Company (BAC) plant, the biggest aircraft manufacturing facility in the world and home of the famous Blenheim and Beaufighter bombers. It also boasted the Rolls-Royce plant, which built Merlin engines for the Spitfires and Hurricanes flown by the RAF. The factories employed hundreds of people locally, and thousands lived in the areas surrounding them.

Four-year-old Betty Allen lived in a terraced house near the BAC, with her parents and two younger brothers. Her father was a painter and decorator, and now also an ARP warden. He took his new duties very seriously, even though the neighbours mocked him for it. Most of them stayed in bed if the air-raid siren sounded, reasoning that since they were five miles from Bristol city centre they weren't really in harm's way. But Mr Allen insisted his family use the Anderson shelter in the garden, which he had gone to great lengths to decorate and make as cosy as possible. Before he set off for his ARP post in town, he always helped his wife and kids carry plenty of blankets and snacks down to the shelter, before shutting them in and placing a heavy oak table against the door for extra protection.

Mr Allen adored his wife, Eileen, all the more so because she had given up everything to be with him. She was from the prosperous Bird family, who had made a fortune with their famous egg-free custard powder, produced at their factory in Birmingham. As a result, she had lacked for nothing growing up, and had been expected to make a suitable match with a man of similar social standing. Instead, she had decided to do something useful with her life, running off to Bristol to take a job as a children's nurse. It was here that she had met and fallen in love with Betty's father, a lowly painter and decorator from Bedminster. In the eyes of her family, that was bad enough – but worse still, he was already married, and his wife refused to grant him a divorce. The couple were forced to live 'in sin', while passing themselves off as the respectable Mr and Mrs Allen.

Betty's mother was now the black sheep of the family and had been cut off financially. She and her growing brood had to make do on what a painter and decorator could earn in wartime, which wasn't much, since redecorating was not at the top of most people's priority list.

Even before the war, Mr Allen had struggled to make ends meet, thanks in part to his generous and friendly nature. Everyone loved him, but more than a few also took advantage of his generosity, always promising to pay him at a future date that never arrived. Others never received a bill at all, since he could see they were struggling and didn't have the heart to charge them.

Betty's mother never once complained about her reduced circumstances. She and her husband loved each other so much, and loved their children so much, that their household was always a happy one.

Betty had inherited her father's friendly disposition and her mother's nurturing, affectionate nature. She loved nothing more than playing mummies and babies with her favourite toys, a pair of beautifully made twin dolls with porcelain faces.

Just before lunch on Wednesday, 25 September 1940, less than three weeks after the start of the Blitz in London, Filton received its own visit from the Luftwaffe.

Betty was upstairs in the 'nursery', as her mother called the children's bedroom, playing with her dolls as usual. Her game was interrupted by the sound of the air-raid siren, and she reluctantly put her toys away and went downstairs.

She accompanied her mother and little brothers into the Anderson shelter in the garden, and her father made sure they were securely shut inside, placing the oak table against the door before he headed into town to his ARP post.

Little Betty and her brothers didn't mind being in the shelter, since Dad had put mattresses down there and it was always warm and comfortable. She and her siblings snuggled up together, and before long she began to drift off.

At 10 o'clock that morning, eighty German bombers and twenty support planes had begun taking off from

France to head across the Channel. Their target was the BAC works at Filton, which they planned to hit at lunchtime, when they hoped the British defences would be slackest.

Just over an hour later, the planes were picked up by British radar, and Fighter Command was informed that a raid was on its way in the south-west of England. Two squadrons of RAF Spitfires were scrambled to intercept the German bombers, whose target, it was assumed, was the Westland aircraft factory in Yeovil, which had been hit two months earlier.

At 11.40 a.m., the British realised they had made a mistake and the Spitfires were ordered to change direction. But it was now too late to reach the German planes before they started dropping their bombs.

At the BAC plant, workers were heading out for lunch when they heard the song 'Marching through Georgia' played over the Tannoy, their signal to head into the factory shelters. As the German planes approached Filton, a local anti-aircraft battery began firing at them, bringing one of the bombers crashing down into a field.

One minute before the raid started, some of the Spitfires managed to catch up with the rear section of the bomber formation and brought down at least one aircraft. It was a small victory, however. At 11.48 the German planes reached Filton and released 168 bombs.

The raid lasted only forty-five seconds but it caused extensive damage to the BAC plant, destroying eight newly minted aircraft along with an important prototype for the new Beaufighter. The RAF engaged the German planes as they left, bringing down five and losing one of their own.

Tragically, several of the factory air-raid shelters received direct hits in the raid, and more than ninety aircraft workers lost their lives. Other bombs missed their target and fell on the surrounding residential streets, killing another forty people and leaving hundreds more injured and homeless. Filton Church had to be turned into a temporary mortuary as the bodies kept piling up.

From their shelter in the back garden, Betty and her family heard the scream of the bombs falling and the terrifying thud of the explosions. Suddenly, there was a deafening bang, and her mother was thrown across the shelter by the blast, landing on top of Betty and her brothers. For a moment everything was lit up by a blood-red light, and then they were plunged into darkness. A terrible rumbling and crashing sound came from overhead, the tin roof shaking and juddering as it was pelted by heavy objects from above.

Betty's mother knew all too well that the sounds were of falling masonry. Their own house was collapsing on top of them. She could only pray that the shelter roof wouldn't give way and crush them. She clutched her children tightly, and they huddled on the mattress together, sobbing in fear as the awful sounds continued overhead.

Finally, when the noise stopped, Mrs Allen crept tentatively to the door. She tried to push it open, but it wouldn't budge. She remembered the oak table her husband always placed against it for safety and pushed a little harder, but still nothing happened.

She and her children were trapped.

Mr Allen had been on ARP duty near the Hippodrome in Bristol town centre when the news came that Filton had been bombed. He instantly left his post and ran as fast as he could the five miles home, terrified that he would return to find his beloved wife and children gone.

When he finally reached their road, a scene of devastation met his eyes. On both sides of the street the houses had been completely wiped out, leaving nothing but rubble where whole families had once lived. Everywhere he looked, flames licked the sky and the air was thick with smoke. Fire engines and ambulances tore past, their bells ringing frantically, while cars drove by with casualties strapped to their roofs. Their tyres had burst in the raid and they made a strange clattering noise as they sped along.

Betty's father staggered down the street, panting and coughing, towards the Allens' own house. As he approached, he saw that it too was gone. All that remained was the staircase, which now led to nothing but sky. The houses on either side had also been reduced to rubble, and the neighbours who had stayed inside them now lay dead beneath the broken bricks.

Mr Allen scrambled over the wreckage of his bombed-out home, trying desperately to reach the garden at the back. His eyes scanned the dirt for the outline of the Anderson shelter, but it had been completely covered with debris. At the back of the garden, a yawning crater marked the spot where a bomb had landed.

Frantically, he began digging with his bare hands, hauling away bricks, tiles and dirt till his fingers bled. 'Eileen!' he shouted. 'Eileen! Can you hear me?'

There was no reply, but he carried on, determined to get his family out, dead or alive.

Deep beneath the rubble, Betty and the others were still huddled together on the mattress, imprisoned in their shelter. The children were crying and clinging to their mother, and she was weeping now too. How long would it be before the air in the shelter ran out and they all suffocated?

Mrs Allen had almost given up hope of them ever getting out, when suddenly they heard Mr Allen's desperate shouts. 'Dad!' the kids screamed. 'Dad! We're down here!'

Hearing them, Mr Allen redoubled his efforts, making it down to the old oak table which he had placed in front of the shelter earlier that day. With one last superhuman effort he heaved it to one side and threw open the door. There was his family, unscathed amidst the devastation all around, saved by the big oak table. They ran to each other, hugging and crying tears of relief.

But as far as little Betty was concerned, not everyone in the family had been rescued. Her twin dolls must still be in the nursery where she had left them.

As the Allens climbed back over the rubble of their house, Betty broke away and ran towards the teetering staircase that was all that remained of their former home.

Her father raced over and caught her just as she reached the bottom step.

'You can't go up there,' he told her.

Betty squirmed in his arms. 'I want to get my dolls!' she cried.

'There's nothing there any more,' her father told her, pointing to the empty space at the top of the stairs.

While her parents scoured the bombsite for any possessions that could be salvaged, Betty stood and sobbed. All around her, people cried for the dead and wounded. But her tears were only for her twin baby dolls, lost forever at the top of the stairs.

Now homeless, the Allens were evacuated to Chew Magna, a village to the south of Bristol, where they were placed in the house of a middle-aged couple with no children. It was a large property, with plenty of room, but their hosts clearly resented having to share it. The bombed-out family were unwanted guests and the couple made no effort to hide their feelings. Nor did they hide their evident disdain for a family they considered 'beneath' them. Little did they know one of their guests was a former heiress.

The Allens lasted barely two months in Chew Magna before the situation there became untenable. Betty's parents decided they would have to leave, setting off with their three children and scant possessions with no idea where to go next.

Fortunately, a neighbour took pity on them and offered them a wooden shed at the end of his garden. In desperation, Betty's parents took it. The family had just one bucket to use as a toilet and another to fetch water from a tap up the hill, but they were grateful to have a roof over their heads.

It was freezing cold in the shed, but Mr Allen gave the children his overcoat as a blanket and they snuggled up underneath it, happy, as ever, just to be together.

Before long, the council found the Allens accommodation in Portishead, a small town to the west of Bristol. They were told they would be getting a detached house overlooking the sea, with three bedrooms, so Betty would have a room to herself. She couldn't wait.

But when the family arrived, they discovered they were staying in Redcliffe Bay, known to the locals as 'The End of the Journey' since it was the last stop on the bus out from Bristol. The place where they were to live was nothing more than a Nissen hut, one of four with a shared toilet, formerly used by the army and more recently squatted by homeless people. The council had cleared the huts out and was now charging families eight shillings to rent them, no small sum to the Allens.

Undeterred, Mr Allen put his painting and decorating skills to good use, turning the hut into a home. He squared off the curved roof on the inside, so that it felt more like a real house, and made sure everything was plastered and freshly painted. Meanwhile, Mrs Allen made woollen carpets and rag rugs to cover the bare floors. By the time they were done, Betty could barely believe it was the same place.

Betty was thrilled to have a bedroom to herself, especially since it boasted one of the only two windows in the hut. She still missed her twin dolls, but her mother, knowing there was no money to replace them, made two little rag dolls for her instead, and her father knocked together a pram for them from some old bits of wood and broken wheels. The rag dolls didn't have the beautiful porcelain faces of her old ones, but she loved them anyway.

To the children, life in Redcliffe Bay felt like a big adventure, even though they could see the planes flying past up the Bristol Channel on their way to bomb the city. 'Is it a German one, Mummy?' Betty would ask, as they rushed to the nearest shelter.

They were within walking distance of the beach and loved going for a paddle and seeing what washed up after a raid. Some days, they pulled scraps of burst barrage balloons out of the water, which Mum sewed into squares to serve as undersheets in case the kids wet their beds.

In Portishead, the war seemed far away, and for little Betty, the most pressing issue of the day was starting school for the first time. The local Catholic school had the best reputation, so her parents decided to send her there, even though she had been brought up Church of England.

The biggest challenge was getting used to going to confession. In the midst of a war against fascism, with adults blowing each other up on her doorstep, five-year-old Betty was called to confess her 'sins' each week.

'What can I say I've done?' she asked her mother anxiously, racking her brains for a minor misdemeanour that would satisfy the priest.

Eventually, her parents decided she would be better off at a Church of England school, and she happily switched to St Barnabas in Redcliffe Bay. A small school with just one room partitioned into infants and juniors, it was doing its best to accommodate evacuees from the London Blitz, who stood out like a sore thumb with their Cockney accents and government-provision jumpers.

Betty made friends easily, but lunch breaks were the hardest time for her. Not because she had no one to sit with but because she often didn't have any dinner money.

'Can I pay tomorrow?' she would ask the dinner lady shyly, when she didn't have enough to cover her food. Sometimes, she and her brothers would pick bluebells and sell them on the side of the road to make a few pennies.

Since moving to Portishead, Betty's father had lost all his previous painting and decorating clients and was struggling to find work. Establishing himself in a new area was proving difficult, and the family finances were looking increasingly dire.

In desperation, Betty's mother did what she had to, to keep her family from going hungry. Mr Allen had saved the family once before, and now it was her turn. She and her husband began going to the pub in the evenings, leaving Betty in charge of her younger siblings. When they returned, they were often accompanied by a young soldier, who would disappear into the bedroom with Mum while Dad waited in the living room. The nocturnal visitors would always have gone by the time the kids woke up the next morning.

Betty's younger siblings were already fast asleep when their parents returned from the pub, but as the oldest, she felt it was her responsibility to stay awake until she knew they were safely back home. From her bedroom she could hear the strangers' voices coming from her parents' room, but she remained blissfully unaware of the sacrifice they were both making for the sake of their family.

Over time, as the bombing raids on Bristol ceased, Mr Allen's painting and decorating work picked up, and bit by bit the family got on to a firmer financial footing. Through it all, Betty's parents had remained as in love as ever, and they always made sure they provided a happy home for their children, despite their hardships.

After several years living in the Nissen hut, during which time three more babies came along, the Allens were overjoyed to hear they were being rehoused in a semi-detached council house in Redcliffe Bay. At last they would have a real house again, and even better, it had a front and back garden, three bedrooms, a kitchen with a gas cooker, and an indoor bathroom. They would no longer have to share a toilet with three other families – and for the first time since being bombed out, they would have stairs again. Eileen was over the moon.

The family was settled in their new home when news came that Reg's former wife had died. At last he was free to marry his beloved Eileen and make their family official.

With their six children in tow, they headed to a local hotel for a modest ceremony, in which Reg and Eileen finally became Mr and Mrs Allen for real.

8

AUDREY

On 24 November 1940, twelve-year-old Audrey Hodges was getting ready for the night of her life. Her favourite comedian was due to perform at St Mary on the Quay in her hometown of Bristol, and she was determined not to miss him.

Audrey had been introduced to Jack Warner thanks to the BBC radio comedy show *Garrison Theatre*, in which he arrived each week on a bicycle shouting his famous catchphrase, 'Mind my bike!' Now, she was keen to add his signature to her already bulging autograph book. Her parents ran a grocery shop not far from the Hippodrome, and as a result Audrey's book already boasted autographs from visiting stars such as Stan Laurel and Oliver Hardy, who often popped in after curtain-down to buy cigarettes.

It was rare for the Hodges family to have a night out together. So rare, in fact, that Audrey's mother had taken the unprecedented step of buying a new coat for the occasion, at her husband's suggestion. He knew that she never spent a penny on herself and was scrupulous about living within their means, but that weekend he urged her to take £10 from the till and treat herself. Mrs Hodges had taken his advice and gone down to Union Street, where an exquisite musquash coat hung in the window of one of the shops. Her budget didn't quite stretch to that, but with a bit of haggling she managed to emerge from the shop a few minutes later with a perfectly serviceable fox-fur coat instead. As she left, though, she couldn't help looking back longingly at the musquash and wishing it could have been hers.

On Sunday night, Mr and Mrs Hodges set off with Audrey, her younger sister Cynthia, and Audrey's friend Hazel. Audrey, too, was wearing her best coat – a knee-length, wool-nap one in navy blue with a matching beret. She felt very grown-up and was determined not to be seen walking with her parents, so she and Hazel went off ahead.

Just as the girls reached the church, the air-raid siren sounded. They hurried inside, joining the rest of the crowd down in the converted crypt where the performance was due to take place.

Audrey and Hazel took their seats and waited excitedly for the show to start, barely registering that the doors had been locked behind them and that her parents and sister hadn't made it into the building in time. They were too busy giggling and imagining what Jack Warner would look like in the flesh.

After a while, a man came on to the stage and announced that the star of the show had been held up but that he was on his way. There were a few groans from the audience, but everyone expected the all clear to sound before long and the evening to unfold as planned.

As time ticked by, though, there was no sign of Jack Warner and his bicycle. The crowd began to get restless. 'What's going on here?' one man demanded. Another got up and tried to leave but was told no one could exit the building.

The talk in the room grew heated, as people started to question why they were being kept inside, and what might be happening up above them. Down in the crypt, they were unaware that a major raid was taking place, and fires were already burning throughout the city.

Audrey and Hazel were still thinking only of Jack Warner, clinging to the hope that sooner or later he would arrive and the show would go on. But after several hours even they had begun to lose faith. Eventually, it became obvious that the night's promised entertainment wasn't going to happen after all. The girls were devastated.

Audrey went up to the man who had made the announcement earlier. 'When can we go home?' she asked him.

'As soon as we get the all clear,' the man told her.

Audrey could do nothing but rejoin the disgruntled crowd and wait it out.

It was morning by the time the doors of the crypt were finally thrown open and the exasperated occupants were allowed to leave. Audrey and Hazel were jostled outside and were immediately hit by the acrid smell of smoke. As they looked up at the sky they saw that fires were still raging all around, while the ground was crisscrossed by fire hoses.

During the night, 134 German bombers had dropped thousands of incendiaries and more than 1,500 tons of high explosives on the city. Within an hour, 45 large fires had started, and the main shopping area around the High Street, Castle Street and Wine Street had been turned into a raging inferno. Many of Bristol's most historic buildings had been gutted, including the seventeenth-century Dutch House and St Peter's Church, the lead roof of which had melted in the heat and slid into the river below. The water mains had been damaged in the raid, causing supplies to run out by 11 p.m. and hampering attempts to quell the flames.

As the rest of the crowd hurried off to find out whether their homes were still standing, the two girls were left to navigate the burning city streets alone. Shouted at by air-raid wardens to avoid this road or that, they soon became disorientated, taking an unfamiliar route and finding themselves running past a burning sweet factory. The fires were raging so violently that Audrey had to pull her beret down over one side of her face to protect her from the heat. She prayed that no sparks would land on her wool-nap coat and set her alight.

The childish concerns of the last few hours had evaporated, and for the first time in her life, Audrey felt pure fear. Would her home have been engulfed in flames too? And what on earth had happened to her parents and little Cynthia?

As Hazel ran off in the direction of her own house, Audrey turned the corner into her road and saw with relief that their house was still standing, although there was a dark hole in the roof where an incendiary had burned its way through.

There was no one at home, so Audrey waited nervously outside, pacing up and down the street. Ever since war had been declared the previous year, her mother had been convinced that a bomb would come for her sooner or later, fearing that she would be robbed of the chance to watch her daughters grow up. Had Mrs Hodges's dire prediction finally come true?

Then Audrey saw three familiar figures turn into the road. '*Mum!*' she cried in relief, running over to them. 'Where have you been?'

Mrs Hodges explained that when the siren sounded they had run to the nearest shelter, inside Georges & Co. brewery, where they had spent an anxious night wondering what had become of Audrey and Hazel. She was extremely relieved to hear that the girls had been safely locked in the crypt all night, with no greater worry than the whereabouts of their favourite radio star.

Mr Hodges went to inspect the damage to the roof. He was very pleased to discover that the precaution he had taken of lining the attic of the house with corrugated iron had proved effective and had prevented the fire bomb from setting the whole building alight. All that was left of the incendiary was the burnt-out casing, which he clutched victoriously as he emerged, and which from that day forth sat proudly on the mantlepiece as a memento.

It wasn't until the following day that Mrs Hodges and the girls ventured out to see what was left of the city centre. Wandering along Union Street, they came to the shop where Audrey's mother had bought her £10 coat in preparation for their big night out. The front window had been shattered and the more expensive musquash coat she had admired had been drenched in water from a fire hose. It now looked for all the world like a drowned cat.

'That coat could have been mine!' Mrs Hodges sighed.

It was a full week before the sodden garment was finally removed from the shop. Mrs Hodges passed by it many times, lamenting what had become of it.

Lusting after expensive clothes was quite out of character for Audrey's mother. As a country girl from Somerset, Vicky Dibble had known what it was to struggle. Her father had died when she was just fifteen, forcing her mother to sell the family shop. Along with her sister, Vi, she had come to Bristol as a teenager in search of work.

Vi had got a job as a waitress, but Vicky – who was shier, and had a dark red birthmark on her face – had been consigned to making tea at the back. She met Fred Hodges at church one day, and noticing the soft pigskin gloves on his hands, recalled a piece of advice her mother had given her: 'Marry a man with money and your children will never go to bed hungry.'

Vicky's instincts about Fred turned out to be correct. His family were respected wine importers, whose cart and horse were a familiar sight around Bristol. Soon, Fred was a familiar sight at the café where Vicky and Vi worked too, turning up with flowers for his new sweetheart.

When Vicky fell pregnant with Audrey, Fred wasted no time in marrying her. They bought a house in the attractive Georgian neighbourhood of Montague Hill, and their future together looked rosy.

But not long after baby Audrey was born, the Great Depression hit. One day Fred's father took him aside and told him the bad news: there was no longer a place for him in the family firm. As the youngest son, Fred had been the last in, and now he would have to be the first out.

Fred had only ever worked for the family business, and he didn't know what to do with himself. His wife urged him to go down to the Labour Exchange, but all they had was a job as a door-to-door salesman, selling papier-mâché bowls on commission. Fred tried his best, but by Friday, when she asked what he had made that week, all he could show for his efforts was half a crown.

'That's not enough,' exclaimed Mrs Hodges. 'We've got a baby to feed!'

But Audrey's mother wasn't one to give up easily. She took the money, put baby Audrey into her pram, and marched down to the local confectionery wholesalers.

'I want to open a shop,' she told the man there, handing over the half a crown Fred had made, in exchange for a large box of assorted sweets.

Back at home, she put a table in the window of the front room and laid out her wares. Then she got a piece of paper, wrote 'SHOP OPEN' on it in big letters, and stuck it above the door.

From that moment on, every waking hour of Mr and Mrs Hodges's lives had been devoted to their new business. Audrey's mother might not have managed to marry a man with money after all, but she was going to make darn sure that her children never went to bed hungry.

By the time Audrey's little sister, Cynthia, was born, the business was thriving. In addition to sweets, the Hodgeses had begun selling sugar, lard, butter, bread and cakes. When Mrs Hodges realised the railings outside the window were perfect for hanging parsnips on, she decided to branch out into vegetables as well.

Mr Hodges still considered himself too much of a gentleman to drag the handcart to the fruit and veg market each week, preferring to hide behind his newspaper and let his wife go instead. But the pair of them worked hard together, keeping the shop open from 8 a.m. till midnight every day. Eventually they were doing well enough that when the house next door came up for sale they were able to buy that too and expand the business.

But while the shop became more and more successful, Audrey and Cynthia were increasingly left to shift for themselves. Their parents were so busy working that the little girls rarely had a proper meal cooked for them, and Audrey often suffered from hunger pangs.

'There's all the food you could want in the shop,' her mother told her. 'Just help yourself.'

As a result, Audrey's diet largely consisted of lettuce,

apples, bananas and grapes, since those were the only items she could reach. At her primary school, everyone else brought homemade jam sandwiches in for their lunch, but Audrey only had an apple to munch on. Her clothes were never laid out for her in the mornings, and if she needed clean underwear she would usually have to rifle through a pile of recently washed laundry, which her mother never got around to ironing.

Audrey always went to school with her dark brown hair looking untidy. She envied the two girls in her class whose mothers worked as dressers at the Hippodrome, and who always sent them in looking immaculate, with their blonde locks lovingly curled and tied up in ribbons. They were the ones the teacher sat at the front of the class, while Audrey was put at the back.

At home, Mr Hodges was keen to teach his daughter the value of money. Audrey learned to count with coins that her father instructed her to put into little piles according to their denomination. As soon as she could write, she was sent down the road with a slate and a piece of chalk, to note down how much their competitors were charging so that he could adjust his prices accordingly.

Other than that, Audrey's parents had little time to impart much knowledge about the world to their daughter. Instead, she gleaned as much as she could from the conversations she overheard in the shop while sitting on the stairs.

Late one evening, in the mid-1930s, some German sailors came in to buy cigarettes. Audrey heard one of them chatting to her mother about the possibility of another war breaking out.

'What *is* war?' Audrey asked Mrs Hodges the next morning.

'Oh . . .' her mother replied distractedly. 'It's to do with soldiers and sailors.'

Intrigued, but not wanting to disturb her mother further, Audrey went away to mull over her answer.

One advantage of having busy parents was that she could wander wherever she wanted in the city without fear of punishment, so she took herself down to the local barracks and approached a soldier at the gate.

'Are you from the war?' she asked him.

The soldier laughed. 'Not yet!'

A few years later, with a new war looking increasingly likely, Audrey's father volunteered as an ARP warden at the nearby Bristol Royal Infirmary. One day he came home with a box containing a strange rubber mask, which he put over his face.

Audrey laughed. She thought it made him look like a monkey.

'What is that?' she asked her father between giggles.

'It's for the gas,' Mr Hodges replied.

The only gas Audrey knew about came out of the stove, and she couldn't fathom why her father would need a mask for that.

Next he put a bucket of sand in the back garden, explaining that it was 'for the bombs'.

Audrey stared at it, wondering how on earth they were expected to catch a bomb in a bucket.

Audrey was far more interested in the Anderson shelter her father had built out back, which soon became the perfect Wendy house for her and Cynthia – a place for them to play shop in, and a home for their dollies.

The years passed, and in the autumn of 1940, finally the bombs came to Bristol. The terrible raid of 24 November, which claimed over 200 lives, was followed by two further heavy attacks in December. King George came to visit what little remained of Castle Street in an attempt to boost morale.

The new year brought with it a vicious attack on the city's docks by a swarm of 178 bombers, in a raid lasting more than twelve hours, one of the longest endured by civilians in the whole war. In March, the fifth heavy raid on the city saw German bombers mistakenly dropping part of their load over the densely populated Easton area, causing 257 fatalities – the worst loss of life in any raid on the city. When Churchill visited the area, morale was so low that local women booed and shook their fists at him.

The conversations Audrey overheard while sitting on the stairs now were anything but child's play. 'There were severed limbs everywhere,' she heard her father tell her mother one morning, when he returned from a shift with the ARP. 'We couldn't let anybody out of the shelters until we'd cleared the pavements.'

Another night, she overheard him tearfully telling her mother how he had been unable to stop a woman going back into her house to rescue her life savings during a raid and had stood helplessly listening to her screams as she was engulfed by flames.

At one scene he attended in Stokes Croft, a whole family had been crushed to death when a wall of their house had collapsed on top of their Anderson shelter. After that, Mr Hodges decided that the next time the siren went his wife and children should go to the convent across the road, which had opened up its basement to the public.

The nuns gave the girls steaming cups of Bovril, which Audrey found absolutely revolting. But she drank it anyway to keep herself warm.

As others came into the shelter, they would bring news of what was happening outside, calling out the names of families who had been hit. One night, Audrey was trying to swallow her disgusting drink when a man came in and announced, 'The King family are all gone.' A murmur went around the room.

Audrey couldn't believe it. Iris King was in her class at school – an annoying ginger-haired girl who always brought up the fact that her older brother was a policeman when it looked like she was going to lose a fight. Audrey had never liked Iris, but the idea that she and her whole family had just been wiped out was hard to comprehend. How could the God her father made her worship at church every Sunday allow such a thing to happen? Audrey remembered that Iris had hit her once, and fleetingly wondered if that was why this fate had befallen her.

The next time the siren sounded, Audrey was on her way to the convent when a plane zoomed past overhead, so low that she could see the pilot inside. There was a swastika painted on the fuselage.

Seeing one of the enemy who had killed Iris and her family, Audrey was suddenly filled with hatred. 'You shouldn't be doing this!' she shouted up at the plane as she ran into the shelter. 'We don't like Germans!'

One morning, the Hodges returned home after an air raid to find the police waiting outside their house.

'A bomb fell in the garden,' an officer informed them. 'The blast's gone through the shop and blown out the back windows.'

Audrey's parents were horrified. The butter, lard, cheese and bacon were all kept on marble slabs at the back of the shop, covered in damp muslin cloths to keep them fresh overnight. They rushed inside, and gasped when they saw their precious produce covered in glass shards.

A local official came to assess the damage and decreed that the food would have to be destroyed. Mr Hodges nodded in agreement, but once the man had gone he made his own assessment. The butter, he thought, wasn't too far gone – only the top half was peppered with glass, while the bottom remained relatively untouched.

The thought of throwing away good produce was anathema to Mr Hodges. He took a cheese wire and sliced off the top of the butter, throwing that away while keeping the rest hidden under the counter. When his customers came in that week, he would whisper, 'I've got some extra butter for you!' and to their delight serve them off the ration from his secret stash.

Audrey hated her school with a passion, so she wasn't sorry in the least when a bomb dropped into the graveyard of the church next door and destroyed it. The pupils were evacuated to Torrington in Devon, and she and Cynthia went with them.

When evacuation plans had been made in the lead-up to war, Bristol had not been included, since it wasn't considered a prime target for air raids. But by 1941 things had changed, and increasing numbers of children were being sent away from the city.

Audrey and her sister were sent to stay with a short, round woman with white hair whose two grown-up daughters, as she liked telling everyone, were both in the forces. She took an immediate shine to Cynthia, especially when she discovered how biddable she was. Soon Audrey's little sister was polishing all the brass in the house until it gleamed, and then she was put to work on the silverware. Audrey, however, was less obliging, and failed to endear herself to their hostess. Desperately unhappy, she eventually wrote and begged her parents to let her return to Bristol.

While Cynthia stayed on in Devon, Audrey came home and started at a new school up the hill from her old one. She didn't know a soul there and felt like a fish out of water. It was all she could do to stick it out for the few months until she turned fourteen at the end of the Easter term of 1942, and she left without her school certificate.

Audrey was delighted to be free of school at last, and she was keen to start earning her own money. Rather than join her parents in their grocery shop, she got herself a job as a cashier for Debenhams, going to work on her first day in a smart white blouse and black skirt that she had made herself.

Unfortunately, after accidentally giving a man the wrong change, she was obliged to hand in her notice. It seemed there was nothing for it but to go to work in the family business after all.

By this point, the enterprising Mr and Mrs Hodges had managed to buy up five houses along their street, expanding the original grocery and adding a draper's shop to their collection. After a while, they mooted the idea of Audrey opening yet another shop in one of the buildings and running it for them, although their plans did not involve letting her keep any of the profits.

Determined to blaze her own trail, Audrey decided it was time to branch out on her own. She took herself down to the Labour Exchange to see what she could find.

The lady behind the desk looked her up and down. Audrey was very young, but she was tall, and she didn't look like a girl who would mind getting her hands dirty. 'I might have something for you,' the woman said. 'But you'd have to leave home.'

'I wouldn't mind that!' replied Audrey.

After passing a medical, she received a letter telling her to report to the Downend Homes for Children. Audrey packed her suitcase and caught the bus out to the edge of town, before continuing on foot to the address she had been given. She arrived at a large crescent of identical semi-detached houses, built at the turn of the century to house orphans and paupers' children.

She knocked at the correct door, and a friendly-looking maid answered.

'I'm Audrey Hodges,' she told the girl.

'Oh yes, we're expecting you,' the maid said, smiling. 'Come in. I'm Rose.'

Rose showed Audrey up to a little bedroom where her new uniform was already laid out for her: a plain grey dress with frilled cuffs, a little hat and a pinafore. She showed Audrey how to secure the hat and pinny with napkin pins.

'Breakfast's at six thirty and you're on duty at seven,' she said, and then left Audrey alone.

The following morning, Audrey slept right through breakfast but she made it downstairs in time for the start of her shift.

The house catered for toddlers aged two to three. After being dressed by the staff, the children were sat down in little chairs in the dining room to be given their porridge.

Looking around the room, Audrey was surprised to see that a large proportion of the children were mixed race. One of the other girls explained to her that they were illegitimate babies fathered by black American soldiers stationed in Bristol.

Audrey knew that many a local girl had fallen for the charms of the American GIs, who had livened up Bristol's nightlife with their jazz music and jitterbugging. Although the black troops were housed in separate units from their white counterparts, the American authorities' attempts to keep them segregated outside of camp, as they were back home, had met resistance from local pubs and clubs. As a result, the black soldiers had experienced a new-found freedom in the city, able to drink where they liked and dance with and date local white girls.

But the future prospects of any such romantic relationship weren't good, even if the GI in question survived the war. The couple would have to seek permission to marry from the American Army, which was invariably refused, while bringing a white wife home to the United States would be very difficult at a time when interracial marriages were still illegal in many states.

Meanwhile, young women who found themselves pregnant and alone faced the stigma of being an unmarried mother and the risk of being thrown out of the family home in disgrace. With no benefits system to rely on, many were forced to give up their babies.

It was a heartbreaking situation for all involved, including the young girls like Audrey who ended up caring for the abandoned children. Some of the infants, unsurprisingly, were quite disturbed, angrily throwing their porridge all over the floor, spilling their orange juice and knocking their chairs over.

It was impossible not to feel sorry for the children, and as Audrey got to know them individually, she began to care about them deeply. But the matron was always on the lookout for girls getting too attached, believing it was best not to let a bond develop that would inevitably have to be broken. As soon as she saw a relationship developing, the girl would be sent to work with a different group of children. After just a month with the toddlers, Audrey was moved to a house along the crescent that catered for three- to five-year-olds, and from there to a house for babies.

Although she had enjoyed looking after the older children, Audrey adored the babies. She soon got to know which of them liked to be sung to sleep, which preferred to be rocked and which liked to be stroked gently on the cheek as they drifted off.

But the job was also distressing. New GI babies were arriving all the time, brought in by distraught young mothers. Audrey had to take a two-day-old baby off its mother's breast, while the woman explained tearfully, 'I would keep it, but I can't give up work.'

Then there were the babies who were brought in by the police, having been abandoned by their mothers in public places. One day, Audrey was on duty when an officer knocked on the door with a tiny baby wrapped in a blanket.

'We found him at Temple Meads Station,' the officer told her as he handed over the little bundle. 'The mother jumped off the train, put the baby in a bin and got back on again.'

The tradition at the children's home was that whichever girl opened the door to the police when they brought round an abandoned baby had the honour of naming it.

'Well, if that's all we know about him, it has to be T. Mead,' Audrey said. 'And the T can stand for Tony.'

Audrey gave little Tony all the love and care she could, despite the matron's edict – just as she did with all the other children she looked after.

Following the war, a nursery school opened for the Downend children in the former Frenchay Hospital. By then, Audrey had qualified as a nursery teacher, and she was delighted to find that her first cohort was the same group of babies she had taken care of when she started at Downend.

The children didn't remember her any more, but she remembered each and every one of them and was happy to have them in her life again.

A few years later, when Audrey married a young soldier she had met at a dance, all her bridesmaids were children from Downend.

9

DOREEN

No one believed the German bombers would make it as far as Northern Ireland, so despite having the highest population density in Britain, Belfast had the lowest proportion of public air-raid shelters, no searchlights, no smoke screen and no Observer Corps.

By spring 1941, there had been more than fifty 'red alerts' in the city, but all of them had turned out to be false alarms. Hardly anyone paid much attention any more, but Doreen Henry's father was the exception. A devoted member of the ARP, he wore his navy-blue boilersuit and tin hat with pride.

Aged almost three, Doreen thought her father looked wonderful in his uniform. But most of the neighbours just laughed when he tried to tell them what to do. Even his own wife had baulked when he returned from his first ARP meeting with a roll of clear tape and insisted on sticking it all over the windows to prevent them shattering in the event of an explosion.

'I won't be able to clean the glass!' Mrs Henry protested. 'Whatever will the neighbours think?'

'What would you rather have – dirty windows or death by flying glass?' retorted her husband, setting to work.

An insurance man by profession, Mr Henry was used to considering the worst-case scenario. He was a volatile man, who veered between moments of boundless enthusiasm and periods of crippling despair. In one of his upbeat moods he had applied to join the air force, only to be rejected for being too old. Now, he was determined to do his bit for the war effort in other ways, whether that was volunteering for the ARP or 'digging for victory' in his back garden.

Sadly, Mr Henry's attempts to grow his own produce were soon thwarted by slugs. Demoralised, he abandoned his vegetable patch, but his loss was Doreen's gain. A few days earlier, she and a few of the other neighbourhood kids had been fascinated to see a hearse making its way down their street, and had followed it all the way to the local cemetery. There, they had watched entranced as the coffin was carried out in front of a crowd of mourners and finally laid to rest in the ground.

Inspired, Doreen decided to organise a funeral for one of her dolls, using her father's abandoned vegetable patch as a burial ground. After laying the little body to rest, she and her friends stood around the grave, pretending to cry.

Doreen had a feeling that someone ought to say something at this point. Fortunately, one of the other girls soon stepped forward. 'Ashes to ashes, dust to dust,' she said solemnly, before adding, 'If the women don't get you, the whiskey must.'

Mr Henry never discovered the body buried in his back garden. If he had, he would no doubt have given Doreen a good smack, as he usually did when she displeased him. In his better moments he could be a fun, playful father, but on his bad days he had a violent temper. In the past, he had hit Doreen simply for making a noise, and he was always telling her what a 'nasty' child she was. Mrs Henry didn't dare intervene, and always did as her husband told her.

As a result, Doreen grew up a shy, unconfident girl, forever trying – and failing – to please her father. She found solace in the companionship of her black-and-white terrier, Toby, who licked away her tears whenever he discovered her crying.

Another source of encouragement was her beloved grandmother, who lived on the other side of the city, along with her Auntie Teenie, Uncle Jim and their daughter, Betty. A tiny old woman who wore her long silver hair in a bun, Granny would cuddle Doreen tightly by the fire and whisper to her that she was her favourite grandchild. She lived in the Shankill Road area in the north of the city, a poorer area than Doreen's middle-class enclave in East Belfast.

Granny had come to Doreen's rescue when a lady had turned up at her house one day with gas masks for the family, insisting they must practise putting them on once a week. The child-size mask had red 'ears', and the lady had tried to convince Doreen it would be fun to pretend she was Mickey Mouse. But as her mother put the mask over her head, her hair got caught in the strap and she screamed.

'Here, let me,' said the lady, grabbing Doreen roughly and yanking the mask over her face, twisting her neck in the process and only making her scream louder.

Mrs Henry dutifully tried to get Doreen to put the mask on again the following week, but Doreen was nowhere to be found. She eventually discovered her hiding under the stairs, and at the sight of the horrifying Mickey Mouse ears the little girl began screaming blue murder.

Luckily, at that moment Granny appeared and demanded to know what was going on. When Mrs Henry explained that she had been given orders to practise putting on the mask every week, Granny snorted. 'That's a lot of nonsense!' she exclaimed. 'You'll only distress the poor girl.'

From then on, the horrifying mouse mask was kept in its box, never to be brought out again.

On the night of 7 April 1941, Doreen was fast asleep when she felt herself being lifted out of her cot and carried down the stairs in her mother's arms. She was placed on an eiderdown in the cubbyhole under the stairs next to Toby the dog, who was whimpering. 'Don't move till I come back,' Mrs Henry said.

When she had gone, Doreen crawled to the entrance of the cubbyhole and peeped out. She saw her father standing by the front door in his ARP uniform, hugging her mother close.

'Will we ever see each other again?' she heard her mother ask him.

'I hope so,' replied Mr Henry, giving her a kiss.

Doreen didn't understand. What could stop her parents seeing each other again?

She watched as her father opened the front door and went outside. Through the open doorway, Doreen caught a glimpse of the sky lit up red behind him. There were strange flashes in the distance and a horrible rumbling sound seemed to be coming from overhead. She retreated inside the cubbyhole again.

When her mother returned and crawled inside, there were tears running down her cheeks. Doreen had never seen her cry before, and instinctively threw her arms around her. 'Don't worry, Mummy,' she said. 'Daddy will chase the naughty noises away.' Then she cuddled up to her mother and went back to sleep.

While Doreen dozed, the thing no one except her father had believed possible was finally happening to Belfast: a German bombing raid.

Compared to the bombardment of London or Birmingham, it was small fry. Just eight bombers dropped explosives on the Newtownards Road, Templemore Avenue and Albertbridge Road areas, while around 800 incendiaries set off fires in the docks. Designed to test the city's defences, which were still woefully inadequate, the night raid became known as the Wee Blitz.

Wee as it was, the raid was enough to convince the government that Belfast was now a serious target for the Luftwaffe. One consequence of this was that the authorities decided all dangerous animals in the city's zoo must be put down immediately, in case it was bombed and they escaped. More than thirty animals, including two polar bears, a black bear, a tiger and six wolves, were shot.

Doreen, who adored animals and had been a regular visitor to the zoo, cried for hours thinking about the poor dead creatures. At least the elephants had been deemed unlikely to be a threat to the public. A baby Asian elephant called Sheila was even lucky enough to spend her nights being looked after in the zookeeper's own home. She and her handler became a familiar sight walking home together each afternoon, stopping at a local shop for a piece of stale bread for the little elephant to chew on.

Doreen might have been able to doze through the Wee Blitz, but the attack that followed on 15 April would have roused even the soundest of sleepers. It was Easter Tuesday, and the Henry family had just returned from a camping holiday in the Mourne Mountains. Doreen was fast asleep when the siren went at 10.40 p.m., and once again she felt herself lifted out of her cot by her mother and carried down to the little cubbyhole under the stairs. Toby the dog was already in there, howling.

'Stop it, Toby!' Doreen told him, but her words didn't make any difference.

Confident that her father would chase away the 'naughty noises' again, Doreen cuddled up to her mother. Mrs Henry insisted on switching off the torch in order not to waste the battery, so the two of them were plunged into total darkness.

Suddenly, there was an almighty crash and the cubby-hole shook violently. Doreen screamed and her mother clutched her tighter than ever. Doreen could feel her trembling, and when she put her hands up to touch her mother's face, she realised it was wet once again with tears.

'The house must have been hit,' Mrs Henry said nervously.

Doreen began to cry too, and they lay there together shaking with fear, as overhead the deafening drone of aircraft engines and the whine of falling bombs continued.

This time, almost 200 Luftwaffe bombers were attacking the city's military and manufacturing facilities, dropping 674 high-explosive bombs, 29,000 incendiaries and 76 parachute mines.

During a lull in the raid, Mrs Henry took the torch and crept gingerly out of the cubbyhole to see if their home was still standing. Doreen waited anxiously in the dark with the whimpering Toby.

'The house hasn't been touched!' she told Doreen in astonishment when she returned. 'But oh God, pity those who have been bombed . . .'

The two of them cuddled up together again, spending the rest of the night holding each other and praying until the all clear came.

Mr Henry, meanwhile, had been out all night with the ARP. Finally, all that time spent learning how to do first aid and put out fires was proving worthwhile. Some 15,000 people had been injured that night and 900 killed, the greatest loss of life of any night raid outside of London.

Not only was Belfast poorly defended, it was also totally unprepared for the number of casualties. With room for only 200 in the city's mortuary, two temporary morgues had to be set up in Grove Baths and St George's Market. Body parts that couldn't be identified were buried in mass graves – in a Catholic cemetery if they were found with rosaries.

The following morning, Doreen's father returned from his shift in tears. When he told his wife and daughter that North Belfast, where Granny, Auntie Teenie and the others lived, had been badly hit they were both worried sick, but Mrs Henry insisted the three of them sit down and eat a good breakfast together.

They were just finishing up when Doreen's Auntie Carrie and Uncle Willie, who also lived on the other side of town, burst through the door. Auntie Carrie was in a terrible state, soaked through and shaking, while Uncle Willie was clutching a cage containing their pet budgerigar, Mac.

Their house by the waterworks, he explained, had been all but destroyed by a bomb blast. The two of them, along with their precious pet, had survived by cowering under the staircase. After picking their way over broken glass and debris, they had walked all the way to East Belfast to entrust Mac to Mr and Mrs Henry's care, while they went in search of somewhere to stay.

Doreen was delighted to have a new pet in the house, and she doted on the little bird. But unfortunately Mac never fully recovered from his ordeal. A few days later, he dropped off his perch, dead.

At least Granny was reportedly alive and well. She had refused to join the rush of Shankill Road residents into the hills to avoid the air raid, as well as forsaking the public shelter just around the corner in Percy Street, but somehow she had made it through unscathed. 'I'm not going to let Hitler put me out of my home!' she had insisted.

Instead, she, Auntie Teenie and Betty had squeezed into the old coal hole, while Uncle Jim crawled under the table in the scullery.

Granny's stubbornness turned out to be their salvation that night. The Percy Street shelter, like many others in the city, was poorly constructed, with walls that had never been reinforced. When a parachute mine exploded a few feet away the walls came crashing down, bringing the concrete roof with them and killing everyone inside.

The blast was strong enough to shatter the windows of Auntie Teenie's house on Morpeth Street and blow in the door of the coal hole, which landed on top of Betty, leaving her badly bruised. Uncle Jim, who had witnessed glass shattering all around him from underneath the scullery table, emerged shaken but unharmed.

A few days after the Easter Raid, Mrs Henry put Doreen in her pushchair and the two of them went to have a look at the bomb damage. The sights they saw were enough to traumatise a grown woman, let alone a little girl. Row upon row of houses sliced down the middle, desperate people picking through rubble to save whatever possessions they could, and everything, everywhere, blanketed in dust.

A man climbed up a ladder to salvage items from the upper floor of his damaged house, which was now exposed to the street. With the curved end of a walking stick he successfully pulled down first a chair and then a chamber pot, to the delight of a growing crowd of onlookers below. Encouraged, he hooked the stick round the leg of a wardrobe and yanked. The heavy piece of furniture wobbled ominously.

His wife, watching from below, begged him to get down. 'I've lost enough without losing you as well!' she cried.

'That wardrobe cost good money!' her husband replied. 'We'll need it when we get a new place.'

While his wife covered her eyes, and the crowd held their breath, the man made another attempt to shift the wardrobe. It teetered precariously and then collapsed on to its side, sticking out over the broken edge of the floor. Determined, he pulled it out further and with the help of a group of onlookers managed to lower it to the ground. Everyone breathed a sigh of relief.

But the worst sight of the day was a man standing all alone, staring dumbly at an empty bomb crater. His flat cap and coat were grey with dust, and he stood perfectly still, gaping open-mouthed at the hole in the road.

'Would you look at that poor man there,' a woman whispered to Mrs Henry.

'What happened to him?' she asked.

'He went to check on his mother up the street,' the woman replied. 'When he came back, his house had been flattened, with his wife and four children inside.' She shook her head sorrowfully. 'He doesn't even have their bodies to bury.'

Seeing the devastation all around her, little Doreen finally realised what those horrible noises she had heard from the cubbyhole could do. War had become very real to her.

A few months later, Doreen accompanied her father on a work trip to Dublin. Since his job in insurance required him to travel, Mr Henry was lucky enough to have a car and a petrol allowance. When his work took him to the south, his family often went with him and made the most of the opportunity to do a little shopping at the department stores Clerys and Arnotts.

Since Ireland had remained neutral during the war, any German or Allied forces who accidentally landed in the Republic were held in internment camps. They enjoyed a surprising amount of freedom, with an honour system that allowed them to go out during the day, as long as they gave their word to return at night.

As Doreen and her father were walking along O'Connell Street, they spotted a couple of German soldiers in uniform out for a stroll. Doreen couldn't believe her eyes. These were the men responsible for bombing her home town, yet here they were, wandering around sightseeing!

She turned to her father. 'What should we do?' she asked him earnestly. 'Should we kill them?'

'No!' laughed Mr Henry. 'If we did that, we'd be arrested. And then we wouldn't be able to go home and eat the delicious sausages we're smuggling, would we?'

Doreen couldn't argue with that logic, so she put her plans for murder on hold.

Although officially Mr Henry was in Dublin on business, his frequent trips there doubled as convenient opportunities to indulge in a bit of smuggling across the border. Not only were prices lower in the Republic, but the severe rationing and shortages of goods experienced in the United Kingdom were not being suffered there either.

It wasn't just sausages that he took back to Belfast with him. Clothes, too, could be illegally imported with a little effort. Doreen would cross the border wearing one hat, coat and pair of shoes, and then return a few hours later in completely new ones – the old garments having been discarded in a public toilet before they embarked on the return journey. Her mother always told her to scuff the new shoes up a bit so they wouldn't look too pristine.

The first time they performed this routine, Doreen had been shocked to hear her father tell the border guard he had 'Nothing to declare'. Her parents had raised her not to tell lies, on pain of a beating – but in wartime, it seemed, the rules had become a bit more flexible.

Having a child in the back seat actually made the smuggling game a bit easier. Normally, Mr Henry would stash his illegal meat in the passenger-side footwell, but one time, when a border guard had asked him for a lift into Belfast, he had found himself in a tricky situation. 'Certainly,' he had told the man, deciding to brazen it out. 'Only please keep your feet off the contraband!'

To his relief, the customs official had merely laughed, before moving the parcel onto the back seat. He and his colleagues knew perfectly well that everyone smuggled, he explained. As long as they made an example of someone every now and then, they could afford to turn a blind eye the rest of the time.

One day, with Doreen in the back of the car, Mr Henry decided to try a new approach. Just before they reached the border, he pulled over. Then to Doreen's dismay he told her to hide a packet of sausages under one of her armpits, and a side of steak under the other.

Doreen kept her arms pinned tightly to her sides as the customs official peered inside the vehicle. Then, to her enormous relief, he told her father to drive on.

As soon as they were across the border, she erupted into giggles, allowing the meat to drop onto the seat either side of her.

That evening, in honour of the key role she had played in the smuggling, Doreen was treated to an extra-large plateful of steak and onions.

In 1942, Doreen was thrilled to learn that she was going to be a big sister. She couldn't wait for this new member of the family to arrive and was sure they would be the best of friends.

But when baby Eileen was born with jaundice, Doreen was immediately suspicious.

'Put her back!' she told her mother, convinced that the little girl was Japanese.

'You can't put a baby back,' laughed Mrs Henry.

'She's dangerous!' Doreen insisted.

But for some reason, no one else in the family seemed to take the threat seriously.

Whenever Doreen looked at her, baby Eileen howled in her face. She had been hoping for a new friend and companion, but her little sister didn't seem to like her.

At least, thought Doreen, she still had her trusty dog, Toby, for company. But then one day Toby developed a nasty lump under his tail, and Mrs Henry said she was taking him to the vet. When she returned there was no dog with her.

'Where's Toby?' Doreen asked innocently.

'The vet said he wasn't going to get any better,' her mother told her sadly. 'The kindest thing to do was to put him to sleep.'

Doreen was devastated. Her mother's attempts to soothe her were no use, and hot, angry tears slid down her face. As they fell to the ground, she remembered how Toby had always licked them away in the past, and felt even sadder.

Eventually, Toby's place in the family was taken by a little cat. Like its predecessor, the new pet always seemed to intuit what Doreen needed. One day, when her father was giving her a particularly rough beating, it suddenly leapt onto his back and dug its claws in.

Shocked, Mr Henry let go his grip on Doreen – long enough for her to run out of the house and get away from him.

Although Doreen was below compulsory school age, Mr Henry felt it was time for her to get an education. As the first in his family to go to university, it was important to him that his children be well educated, and to that end he found a private school with an infants' class that she could join.

Doreen was terrified of displeasing her father, and tried her best at her new school. She knew Mr Henry was eager for her to start reading – he had even bought her a book as a birthday present – but no matter how hard she stared at the black squiggles on the page, she just couldn't make sense of them. No one knew it at the time, but Doreen was dyslexic.

Her schoolteacher didn't help much, and nor did she come to Doreen's aid when one of the boys in the class started bullying her. The horrid boy delighted in running a toy pram into her legs over and over again, making her cry. Doreen never told her parents what was happening at school, knowing that they wouldn't show her any sympathy.

Soon she was spending every weekday morning in tears, too anxious to eat her breakfast. As the weeks went by, she became increasingly weak and rundown, and before long she had fallen ill. When she developed an alarmingly high temperature, Mrs Henry called the local doctor, who diagnosed her with scarlet fever. Soon she was in the back of an ambulance on her way to Haypark Fever Hospital.

When she arrived, a stern-looking nurse led her away and plonked her unceremoniously into a bath of lukewarm water mixed with Jeyes Fluid, then proceeded to scrub her furiously with carbolic soap. Doreen cried out in pain, but this only seemed to anger the nurse. 'I'll give you something to cry about!' she said, before giving her a hard slap.

Once the bath was over, Doreen was taken to a ward and dumped in a cot, before the nurse marched out of the room. She peered nervously around at the other cots, all of which were empty, and began to cry.

Day after day went by, and the only person Doreen saw was the dreaded nurse. No one ever came to visit her, and no word came from her parents. She felt sure they had abandoned her forever.

In despair, Doreen stopped eating altogether, and gradually she became weaker. Before long she was so run-down that a gland in her armpit became swollen and turned septic. The nurse was furious that she now had to dress the wound every day in addition to her other duties, and she told Doreen it was her own fault for having refused to eat.

In fact, although Doreen didn't know it, her parents had visited her every day. They weren't allowed into the ward and could only watch her through a small window in the door, which Doreen was unable to see.

Watching their daughter crying her eyes out in her hospital bed every day touched Mr and Mrs Henry's hearts, and they felt sorry for her. To cheer her up, they brought her favourite soft toy from home and asked the nurse to give it to her. It was a pink bunny rabbit, whose ears Doreen liked to suck. Her parents watched through the window as their little girl clung to it gratefully.

After two weeks, the doctors decided Doreen did not have scarlet fever after all – only a bad case of tonsillitis. They booked her in for a tonsillectomy in a couple of weeks' time and then discharged her.

Mr and Mrs Henry arrived to take her home in their car. But before she left the hospital, the nurse had one last insult to add to injury. She took away Doreen's toy rabbit, telling her that it couldn't go home with her in case it carried infection. Instead, it would have to be sent to the hospital incinerator.

Doreen cried all the way home, distraught at the loss of her little bunny.

'We're so sorry,' said her father, feeling genuinely bad for her. 'If we'd known she was going to do that, we'd never have brought it.'

His attitude towards Doreen seemed to have softened a little. When they got back home, she found a brand-new doll's house waiting for her, and to help her get her strength back after her illness, her father bought her a secondhand bicycle too.

*

The doctor had advised Mr and Mrs Henry not to send Doreen back to the private school that had made her so unhappy. Instead, she was to wait until she reached compulsory school age, and then go to the local primary school.

After an extra-long summer holiday, Doreen started at Harding Memorial School. After her previous experience, she was still feeling a little apprehensive, but her worries were soon dispelled by a girl called Moira, who gave her a big smile and quickly claimed her as a friend. In fact, all the children at Harding Memorial seemed much more friendly than the kids at the private school. Gradually, Doreen relaxed as she realised she didn't need to worry about being bullied any more.

But the biggest difference of all was made by her new teacher, Mrs Armstrong. A kind and conscientious widow, she did her best to encourage all her pupils, and avoided using the cane.

One day, when Doreen wrote the word 'show' back to front in a spelling test, Mrs Armstrong allowed her the mark anyway. 'Don't worry,' she told Doreen kindly. 'I know you know how to spell it.'

Mrs Armstrong also had a different approach to teaching children to read, getting them to sound out a word if they didn't know it. Finally, reading clicked for Doreen, and despite her slow start she soon became an avid bookworm. Much to her father's delight, she began gobbling up as many stories as she could get her hands on.

But more important than giving her a love of reading, Mrs Andrews had restored Doreen's confidence in herself. By the end of the war, Doreen had risen to the top of her class. In her end-of-year exams, she came second out of sixty kids, with the best mark of any of the girls. As a prize, Mrs Armstrong presented her with a book of stories called *My Nicest Book*, which became her most treasured possession.

When Mr Henry heard about his daughter's achievement, he had only one question for her: 'Why didn't you come first?'

But his words couldn't take away from Doreen's triumph. Nothing could dent her new-found confidence now – not even her father.

10

FRANCES

Outside of London, the area around the Liverpool docks was the most dangerous place to live in Britain during the war. The city's teeming port and the industrial districts around it had been identified by the government as a prime target for German air raids, and before war had even been declared a huge operation was under way to protect them. Anti-aircraft batteries were installed either side of the River Mersey, as well as a series of pill boxes, gun emplacements, searchlights and barrage balloon launch sites.

Unfortunately, some of the first balloons to be raised above the city were struck by lightning and came crashing down into the river in flames, killing one of their RAF handlers. This inauspicious beginning hardly instilled confidence.

Nevertheless, the barrage balloons soon became a familiar sight in Liverpool, especially in industrial areas such as Vauxhall, which lay just a stone's throw from the docks. It was here that young Frances Twigg had spent the first six years of her life, making the grimy streets around the many factories her urban playground.

Frances and her brothers and sisters had learned to find their fun where they could, stealing sugar off the back of the lorries going in and out of the giant Tate & Lyle factory opposite their flat on Hornby Street, and boiling it up to make toffee. Their mother gladly took some of the spoils to make toffee apples to sell off her fruit cart at Great Homer Street Markct.

Food had to go a long way in the Twigg household, where there were many mouths to feed. Large families were common in the fiercely Catholic community of Vauxhall, but the Twigg family tree had even more branches than most. Mrs Twigg had given birth twenty times, and all but the last two babies, a pair of twins, had survived. She had raised them all in a three-bedroom tenement flat with just one gas light and no electricity, the littlest ones sleeping four to a bed, top-to-toe.

Mrs Twigg was a devout Catholic, but her husband had been raised a Protestant. In order for the priest to agree to marry them, Mr Twigg had been forced to convert, but it was a sacrifice he had been happy to make. With her petite figure and long fair hair coiled in plaits around her head, his bride had been widely considered the most beautiful woman in Vauxhall.

Mrs Twigg could neither read nor write, but she was a natural mother – warm, kind and always ready to offer help to anyone who needed it. Her advice was always sought by the other mums, and if anyone had a problem they were told to 'go and ask Twiggy'. Throughout all her pregnancies, she continued to take her handcart to market each week and never once complained.

Luckily Mr Twigg was never out of work. His family were the proud owners of three barges, so he was always busy ferrying corn, peanuts and other foodstuffs along the Leeds and Liverpool Canal. But with so many children, keeping them all fed and clothed was still a stretch.

Things got easier as the older Twigg children grew up and got jobs, and one by one began to move out to get married. To the little ones, they were more like uncles and aunts than siblings, and by the time the youngest, George, was three, his oldest brother, John, was well into his twenties, with a wife and six children of his own.

Frances was the second youngest Twigg and very much took after her mother. She was blonde and pretty, and she adored babies. She would regularly knock on the neighbours' doors, begging to take their little ones out in their prams, and the exhausted mothers on the block were only too happy to oblige her.

By the age of six, Frances had spent a year at the local Catholic school, Our Lady of Reconciliation, but she hadn't learned much. The school was run by nuns whose main concern seemed to be instilling as much religious doctrine into their pupils as possible, and the children had nothing to practise their letters with but chalk and slate.

By the summer of 1939, it looked unlikely that the kids would be returning to school in September anyway. A public information leaflet had been distributed via schools and churches detailing the proposed evacuation scheme, naming Liverpool, Bootle, Crosby, Birkenhead and Wallasey among the areas included.

On 1 September, the exodus began, with twenty-five special trains leaving Lime Street Station for the North Wales coast and various other rural destinations. The same day, the *Liverpool Daily Post* ran an article reassuring parents that their children would receive a warm welcome in the countryside, where 'mountains' of biscuits would be waiting for them on arrival. But articles about the evacuation never mentioned specific locations, since newspaper editors had been told to suppress information about where the children were going.

Meanwhile, in Wales, vans with loudspeakers were driving around seaside resorts, urging holidaymakers to go home to make way for the evacuees who would soon be arriving.

There was much excitement in the Twigg household when Frances, Nellie, Thomas and Nancy heard that they were to be among the evacuees. George, who was aged just three, was disappointed to learn he was too young to join them.

Mrs Twigg helped the children pack their belongings in four little haversacks and then gave each of them a brown paper bag of food to last them the day. 'Make sure you all stay together,' she said, hugging each of them tightly.

As Frances boarded the train with her siblings, she felt she might bubble over with excitement. She had never left Liverpool before, and here she was, going on the adventure of her life. The fact that her mother wasn't coming too didn't bother her, since being from a large family she was used to her elder sisters taking care of her.

At Crewe the children disembarked from the train, boarding coaches that would take them to their final destinations. The Twigg siblings made sure they stuck together, as their mother had instructed, and after a short journey they arrived in the little village of Haslington in Cheshire.

There, they were taken to a church hall, where they were to await their host families. Contrary to the newspaper report, there were no mountains of biscuits waiting for them on arrival. Worse still, none of the host families were keen to take on four siblings, so the Twigg children were the last to be chosen.

Eventually, they were taken in by two brothers and their respective families. Frances and Nancy went to stay with the younger Mr Brown and his wife, and Nellie and Tommy with the elder Mr Brown and his wife. The Twigg children might not all be under one roof as their mother had wanted, but at least being within a single extended family meant that they would see each other often.

In any case, Frances and Nancy saw Tommy and Nellie every day at the little village school. Frances settled in well there, and after the meagre education she'd had at Our Lady's, it turned out to be a noticeable improvement. They had pens and paper to write with and teachers who seemed genuinely interested in their progress. Frances's teacher was a Welsh lady called Mrs Evans, who immediately took the little girl under her wing. Soon she was making good progress in her lessons.

Every Friday, one pupil would be named top of the class and rewarded with a penny to spend in the local sweet shop. Frances watched enviously as her classmates took it in turns to buy themselves a bag of liquorice. She assumed it would never be her turn, but to her astonishment, one Friday Mrs Evans called out her name.

The pupils all clapped as the teacher handed Frances the hallowed penny. 'Here you are, you clever girl!' she told her.

Frances couldn't believe it. She'd never been called clever at Our Lady's, or encouraged in any way. Most of the children there had lived in fear of the nuns and the punishments that were constantly meted out.

Triumphant, she ran down to the local sweetshop to purchase her reward. To her disappointment, the shop had run out of liquorice that week, and she had to make do with lemon drops. But the victory still tasted sweet.

While Frances was now excelling at school, her eleven-year-old brother, Tommy, was adjusting less well to their change in circumstances. The older Mr and Mrs Brown were very strict compared to his own parents, and he disliked having to abide by all their rules. Back in Liverpool, Tommy spent most of his free time hanging out on street corners with his little gang of mates, getting up to whatever mischief they wanted. But now when he stayed out late or arrived home with an armful of apples he had scrumped, he invariably found himself in trouble.

He wasn't alone. For many inner-city kids, the move to the countryside came as a huge culture shock, and they struggled with the boredom of life in a rural village. In mid-September, the issue was already being raised in the House of Commons, with the Labour MP for Caernarvon describing how 424 mothers and children from the Edge Hill district of Liverpool had been sent to a little village on the point of the Llŷn Peninsula, and, finding themselves in an area with no pubs and nothing in the way of entertainment, all but fifty had returned home within a matter of days.

Equally, the state of some inner-city children horrified their hosts in rural areas. Reports quickly began appearing in the local press of evacuees from Liverpool and Birmingham arriving sick, dirty and crawling with lice. Some housewives claimed they'd had to burn every scrap of bedding the evacuees had used.

In Frances's host family, things soon took a turn for the worse. One afternoon, the younger Mr Brown came home from work and sat down to eat his dinner. Nancy had just run upstairs to get something when she passed the doorway of her hosts' bedroom and noticed a pipe sitting on the mantlepiece. She recognised it immediately as belonging to Mr Brown's older brother, who often came round to visit during the daytime when his brother was out at work. Trying to be helpful, she brought it downstairs with her and put it on the table in front of her host.

'Your brother left his pipe in your bedroom,' Nancy said innocently.

The younger Mr Brown's fork stopped halfway to his mouth. He stared at the pipe for a moment, then slammed his cutlery down and stormed out of the room.

That night, while Nancy and Frances lay in their beds, an almighty row broke out downstairs.

In the morning, they crept anxiously down to breakfast. To their relief, Mrs Brown was alone in the kitchen, but they were shocked to discover she was furious with them.

'You two are nothing but troublemakers!' Mrs Brown told the two sisters. 'You're not welcome in this house any more. Get out!'

The two girls had no choice but to pack their bags and leave.

Luckily, the school soon arranged for another local family to take them in. To their relief, the Hedges turned out to be much nicer, and for the next year or so, life in rural Cheshire remained relatively peaceful.

The same couldn't be said for what was happening back home. Beginning in the summer of 1940, Merseyside became the most heavily bombed area in the country outside of London. After a series of reconnaissance operations, full-scale air raids began that August, with 150 bombers attacking Liverpool, Wallasey and Birkenhead on the 28th. Three days later, an even heavier raid saw the city ravaged by more than 100 fires. Along the dock road nearly every building was ablaze, while ships, warehouses and the Custom House were on fire too. As fire crews attempted to put out the flames, they were machine-gunned from the air by the enemy.

The bombers returned relentlessly throughout September, shattering the stained glass of Liverpool Cathedral, damaging Everton's Goodison Park football ground and demolishing a wing of Walton Gaol, burying prisoners and guards together under the rubble. Twenty-one bodies were recovered, but the prison governor was convinced there should have been twenty-two and that one of the prisoners had escaped during the raid. It would be eleven years before the missing body was discovered during reconstruction works.

By the night of 26 September, the emergency services were stretched beyond their limits, and reinforcements had to be called in from Manchester, Bolton, Preston and Blackpool. Fires raged in the south docks and warehouses, causing the loss of thousands of tons of food and other goods, while part of the Overhead Railway that ran alongside the docks was damaged when a warehouse wall collapsed on to it.

In a major attack in November, more than 300 enemy planes targeted the city, dropping over 30,000 incendiaries and 356 tons of high explosives, as well as using parachute mines for the first time. One of these landed on a building in Durning Road where around 300 people were sheltering in the basement. Two-thirds of them were either crushed to death or burned when burst gas pipes ignited, in what Churchill called the single worst civilian bombing incident of the war.

After a short respite, the so-called Christmas Blitz saw a three-day raid by hundreds of bombers, causing terrible damage and loss of life. On 20 December, the bombs fell non-stop from 6.30 p.m. to 4 the next morning and fires burned across the city. The Town Hall, Municipal Buildings, Cunard Building and Exchange Station were among the landmarks hit, while fires ravaged the north docks all the way to Bootle. A row of railway arches in Bentinck Street, which were being used as a makeshift shelter, took a direct hit. Concrete blocks from the arches fell on top of the people huddled beneath, killing forty-two of them. The rescue operation took five days.

Frances and her siblings might be safely ensconced in Cheshire, but her eldest brother John's family were right in the thick of it. He lived with his wife, Ellen, and their children in a corner flat in Blackstock Gardens, one of the large 1930s tenement blocks that characterised the Vauxhall area.

At the time of the raid, John was in Formby training with the army, and their youngest child, a baby called Catherine, was in hospital with a chest infection, leaving six members of the family at home in Blackstock Gardens. When the siren went, Ellen hurried to get eighteen-month-old Robert, three-year-old John, seven-year-old Teresa, eight-year-old Ellen Jnr and ten-year-old Mary down to the shelter in the courtyard of the flats.

She was relieved to get all the kids inside the shelter quickly, since it was soon packed with more than 200 people. As the raid began, two trams stopped on nearby

Vauxhall Road to allow their passengers to run inside and take cover, and before long the shelter was so crowded that local residents had to be turned away. They rushed back home, little knowing that they were the lucky ones.

That evening, just five nights before Christmas, the Blackstock Gardens shelter took a direct hit. The concrete roof and brick walls collapsed on top of the terrified people huddled inside.

Rescue workers were soon on the scene, trying their best to dig survivors out of the rubble. Meanwhile, word spread quickly throughout the local area. When Mrs Twigg heard what had happened, she rushed over straight away to find out what had become of her son's family.

She arrived to find John's corner flat had been completely destroyed in the raid. If Ellen and the five kids had stayed at home that night, they would surely all be dead.

All around, rescue workers were scrambling to remove piles of debris, while local people clambered over the rubble, calling out desperately for their loved ones. Mrs Twigg ran frantically from person to person, asking if anyone had seen her daughter-in-law and her grandchildren.

She soon ascertained that Ellen and the kids had been inside the shelter when it was hit. Now there was nothing she could do but wait anxiously to see if they would be pulled out alive.

In time, the rescue workers managed to dig free John's eldest daughter, Mary. She was pulled out coughing and covered in dirt, with a large cut on her head where a pickaxe had accidentally hit her during the rescue effort.

Mrs Twigg threw her arms around her granddaughter, crying with relief, before Mary was taken away in an ambulance.

John, meanwhile, had already heard about the bombing and immediately asked permission to leave his army camp. He arrived at Blackstock Gardens to find his mother standing by the bombsite, her face ashen.

Mrs Twigg broke the terrible news that while Mary had been saved, little Robert, John, Teresa, Ellen and their mother remained unaccounted for, and it was now thought unlikely that there would be any more survivors.

John stared at her in disbelief. 'You're telling me my wife and children are in *there*?' he replied, gesturing at the pile of bricks and masonry that had swallowed up almost his entire family.

Mrs Twigg nodded, her heart aching for her son.

At least baby Catherine had been spared – her life saved, ironically, by the chest infection that had put her in hospital.

John's immediate thought was to be reunited with his other surviving daughter, but no one knew where the ambulance had taken Mary. He spent the next few hours going from one hospital ward to another, searching desperately for her.

At last, he heard a feeble voice cry, 'Dad!' and turned to see her lying in a hospital bed, her head covered in bandages.

He held her to him, shaking with relief. But how would their family ever come back from such a tragedy?

The Twiggs weren't the only family in Blackstock Gardens who suffered multiple losses that night. Many local families were completely wiped out as they sat side by side in the shelter. While the official death toll eventually reached seventy-two, many bodies were never found, and the true figure was thought to be more than 200.

The *Liverpool Echo*, operating under strict wartime restrictions, could only report vaguely: 'A communal shelter was hit and it is feared there are many casualties.'

Despite his grief, John had no choice but to return to the army, leaving baby Catherine with his mother. Mrs Twigg promised to care for her like one of her own.

Ten-year-old Mary, meanwhile, was sent to join Frances and her siblings in Cheshire.

Although technically their niece, Mary was actually a couple of years older than Frances, and the Twigg children quickly accepted her like a new sister. Outwardly, she seemed to have coped with her ordeal well. The only discernible sign of what she had suffered was the two-inch scar on her head. What she felt at being sent away from her father and sister so soon after losing the rest of her family, however, no one knew.

While the Luftwaffe continued targeting Merseyside, the Twigg children remained safe in rural Cheshire. But when Frances's older sister Nancy turned fourteen, she left school and returned to Liverpool to find a job.

Tommy, who had never fully adjusted to life in the countryside, took it upon himself to follow her. One day, instead of going to school, he walked the two miles to Crewe, bought himself a penny platform ticket and hopped on a train home. Despite Mrs Twigg's best efforts, there was no convincing him to return, so he stayed in Vauxhall for the remainder of the war.

With the other two siblings gone, it was decided that Frances and Mary should go and join Nellie, who was still living with the older Mrs Brown. After the incident with the pipe, Frances was reluctant to have anything to do with the family again, but at least now the older Mr Brown had moved out of the marital home and was living with his elderly mother instead.

Mrs Brown had four grown-up children still living at home, and made no attempt to hide her ambivalence about the extra houseguests. She secretly recompensed herself by opening the packages Mrs Twigg periodically sent the girls, helping herself to most of the sweets and other treats before handing them just a few leftovers.

As the months went by, the meals at Mrs Brown's got leaner and leaner too, as their hostess used their ration coupons to feed herself and her own children, while giving the Twigg girls the bare minimum. Often dinner was just a slice of bread each and one cup of tea to share between the three of them, while their evening meal consisted of soup as thin as dishwater. The girls were soon hungry all the time and resorted to supplementing their diet with whatever raw vegetables and fruit they could pluck from the fields of nearby farms.

With another wartime Christmas approaching, Mrs

Twigg came to Haslington to visit her daughters and Mary. Before she returned home, Frances begged her to let them all return for Christmas. But having already lost so many loved ones to the German bombs, her mother was understandably reluctant.

'We'll have to see,' she replied. 'I'm not making any promises.'

Once Mrs Twigg was on the train home, however, the girls relayed the conversation rather differently. 'Mam says we can go home for Christmas!' Frances told Mrs Brown excitedly.

Their reluctant hostess certainly wasn't going to ask too many questions. 'Oh, how nice!' she said, clearly thrilled to be getting rid of them for a couple of weeks.

Frances packed her belongings into an old violin case, which Mrs Brown had given her to use as a suitcase, and Mrs Brown's daughter accompanied the three girls to Crewe Station, where the platform was already thronging with soldiers going home on leave.

A captain came up to the three girls and asked where they were heading.

'We're going home to Liverpool for Christmas!' Frances replied, beaming.

'Alone?' the man asked, looking concerned.

Frances nodded. She, Nellie and Mary were so happy to be leaving that the crowds of young men all around didn't bother them a bit.

'Stay there and wait for me to come back,' the captain told them.

A few moments later, he returned with a young soldier. 'I want you to look after these girls until they get off the train at Liverpool,' he told him. 'That's an order.'

'Yes, sir,' the soldier replied, escorting the three girls on to the train.

So it was that the British Army aided the young Twiggs in going AWOL from Cheshire.

When they arrived at Lime Street Station, the girls thanked the young soldier and told him they could make their way home from there. But as they emerged from the station it was dark and raining, and the bombs had changed the cityscape so much since they had been away that they barely recognised it.

'How are we going to find our way home?' asked Frances, beginning to feel afraid.

Fortunately, Nellie had an idea. 'I know where our street is,' she said. 'We just have to look for the two tunnels going across.'

The 'tunnels' she referred to were the overhead walk-ways belonging to the Tate & Lyle factory opposite the Twiggs' tenement block in Vauxhall. Luckily, the factory was still standing, and with the help of this familiar local landmark the three girls were able to navigate back to Hornby Street.

As they approached the tenements, Nellie had another bright idea. 'Let's give Mam a surprise,' she said, grinning.

She knocked on the door of their flat, and then the girls crouched down and hid behind the landing wall.

Mrs Twigg opened the door. 'Who is it?' she called.

Suddenly all three of them jumped out and shouted 'Hooray!'

'Jesus Christ!' shrieked Mrs Twigg, who very rarely took the Lord's name in vain. 'What are youse lot doing here?'

'We've come home!' shouted Frances, running into her mother's arms.

Over the next couple of weeks, as the girls filled Mrs Twigg in on their experiences in Haslington, the full extent of Mrs Brown's stealing became apparent. It turned out that many of the gifts Frances's mother had sent them, including knickers, socks, lollipops and chocolate, had never been passed on. Their hostess had evidently taken them all herself, and most likely sold them on the black market.

But Mrs Twigg was even more shocked to hear that the girls had been going hungry while the Browns ate well on their rations. 'You're not going back there!' she told them angrily. 'Bombs or no bombs.'

In fact, Mrs Twigg was so outraged at the way the girls had been treated, especially after everything poor Mary had already suffered, that she made it her business to visit Mrs Brown after Christmas and give her a piece of her mind.

Frances was thrilled to be back home, even if it did mean getting used to air-raid sirens for the first time, and nights spent on hard wooden benches in the nearby public shelter. Fortunately, the worst of the bombing was over by now, and there was no repeat of Mary's terrifying experience at Blackstock Gardens.

Returning to Our Lady's, Frances found she now had to share her desk with another girl, since two other local schools had been bombed out while she was away, and their pupils had been absorbed into her own.

Instead of scrumping apples from farmers' fields, Frances now spent her spare time making Wendy houses out of bricks from a bombed-out block of flats behind the tenements or playing on the stairs of a blitzed factory nearby. But she couldn't have been happier.

Mrs Twigg made good on the promise she had made John, giving Mary and her baby sister, Catherine, as much love as she did her own children, and doing her best to fill the void left by their mother's death.

When he was finally demobbed towards the end of the war, her son returned home a broken man. His hair had fallen out, and he now looked much older than his years. While he had been overseas fighting, he hadn't had to deal with the reality of life without his wife and children. Now, the hole they left behind gaped wide open.

Mrs Twigg had secured the flat next door for him and his girls to live in, so that she could keep a close eye on all three of them. To Frances and her siblings, it felt strange when Mary and Catherine finally moved out, since after so many years together the girls had come to feel like extra sisters. But the two households remained so close to each other that they were practically merged into one, and in time, the terrible tragedy they had suffered only served to make their bond tighter.

With the help of the rest of the Twigg clan, John gradually got back on his feet, found a civilian job and proved a steadfast father to his surviving daughters. In time, he remarried and had two sets of twins with his new wife – bringing four more Twiggs into the world to take the place of those he had lost under the rubble of Blackstock Gardens.

11

CLARA

Despite growing up in relative poverty, four-year-old Clara Green's life had always been a happy one. The Greens lived in Toxteth, in the south end of Liverpool, where Clara, her five brothers and sisters and her parents shared a cramped one-bedroom house on Lamport Street.

Mr Green had lost his steady job at the gas company after injuring his leg playing football in his lunch break. He now scraped a living running errands for the carter who lived next door, taking the horse-drawn cart out to sell firewood or crates of fruit.

Money was short, but somehow Mrs Green always managed to put on a good Sunday tea, laying out the threadbare tablecloth and treating the children to biscuits, fruitcake, jelly and custard, all bought 'on tick' at the local shop. Clara and her siblings looked forward to it all week, and the little indulgence helped them cope with the privations on other days.

The children spent most of their spare time outside, playing hopscotch, rounders and skipping with the other neighbourhood kids – and sometimes the local mums too, who joined in, using their washing lines as skipping ropes.

On Saturdays, Clara's oldest sister, Mary, would pile all the younger ones into an old pram and take them to nearby Princes Park, bringing lemonade and sandwiches to keep them going for the day.

The Greens' house was always full of music. Everyone in the family could carry a tune, and Mr Green and Mary were also accomplished accordion players, frequently called upon to play at neighbourhood parties.

Clara adored her father and loved nothing more than sitting on his shoulders and watching the big ships going in and out of the Liverpool docks, which lay just half a mile away from their home. Mr Green wasn't a tall man but he was muscular, and in his arms she always felt safe.

Her mother was a tiny, round woman of Irish descent, shy, gentle and loving. Between them, they created an atmosphere of warmth and security for their six children that more than outweighed their practical hardships.

But in August 1939, less than a month before war was declared, the Greens' safe family bubble was burst forever. In August, Clara's eight-month-old sister Betty came down with a mystery illness that caused her to cry day and night. No matter what Mrs Green did, she just couldn't seem to soothe the poor baby. She and her husband took it in turns pacing up and down with Betty at night, counting the hours until daybreak.

After a string of sleepless nights, they took the baby to hospital, where she was diagnosed with an abscess behind her ear. The doctors operated immediately, but it was too late to save her. Baby Betty came home the next day in a little white coffin.

Friends and relatives visited to pay their respects, peering into the tiny wooden box, which stood on a stand in the front room. Four-year-old Clara couldn't quite see over the top, so one of her aunts lifted her up to let her have a look. There lay the baby sister who had cried so loudly for days, lying eerily still and silent inside.

Of the children, only twelve-year-old Mary was allowed to go to the funeral. Clara and the others watched their parents driving off in the horse-drawn hearse, Betty's little coffin resting on their knees as tears rolled down her mother's cheeks.

Just a week after burying Betty, the Greens had to say goodbye to their three eldest children, Mary, Billy and Rose, who were evacuated to Chester with the rest of their classmates. Mrs Green joined the other mothers waving the children off, still dressed in her black mourning clothes. Clara had never seen her mam look so sad.

Their departure coincided with little Winnie, the youngest, being taken into hospital with chest problems. A delicate child, she was often poorly, but this latest illness couldn't have come at a worse time. To add to the Greens' woes, Clara also came down with a bad case of whooping cough.

From a home full of children, the Greens were now down to just one, and the house felt terribly empty. Clara missed her siblings, especially her six-year-old sister, Rose.

Shy and quiet like her mother, Clara had always relied on her more confident older sister to protect her. Nighttimes were the hardest, when she tried to go to sleep in the room that they had all shared. Rose's kicking and her brother Billy's snoring had always annoyed her, but now she found she couldn't drop off without them. 'I'm not asleep, you know,' her little voice would call down the stairs every evening, after her mother had put her to bed.

In the meantime, Mary, Billy and Rose had arrived in Chester, where they and all the other evacuees had been told to sit in a field and wait to be collected. One by one, the Green children watched their schoolmates being picked up by different host families, until they were the only ones left.

They were just beginning to think no one wanted them when a young couple finally arrived to claim them. The reason they were late, the pair explained, was that they had only just got back from their honeymoon. Doubtless they were not best pleased to find themselves foster parents to three children so early in their married life.

Rose quickly won them over with her bubbly personality, becoming a firm favourite. But while she was taken on special outings with the couple, poor Mary and Billy were left waiting on the front step for their return.

Things only got worse when the couple decided they could no longer cope with three children, and Billy was sent off to a different family. Mr and Mrs Green had told their children to make sure they stayed together, but now

Billy found himself living all alone with strangers. His new hosts were very kind and tried their best to make him feel at home, even going to visit Mr and Mrs Green in Liverpool to reassure them they were taking good care of Billy. But the trauma of being separated from his family affected him profoundly, and he developed a stammer that would stay with him for the rest of his life.

After seven weeks, Mr and Mrs Green went to visit their children in Chester, taking along Clara, who was still suffering with whooping cough. Seeing the toll that evacuation was taking on Mary and Billy, they made up their minds to bring all of them back to Liverpool immediately. War or no war, the Greens were determined to get their family back together.

Soon Clara and Winnie had both recovered from their illnesses, and they were all able to spend a happy Christmas with one another.

By the spring of 1940, things were looking up for the family. Mr Green had a new job with a demolition company and his wife was pregnant again. They had moved into a flat in nearby Northumberland Buildings, a large block of 'labourers' dwellings' built in the 1860s, where for the first time they had two bedrooms and an indoor bathroom.

When she started at St Patrick's School, aged five, Clara got used to taking her little gas mask with her in its cardboard box and being ready to run into the shelter in the playground whenever the air-raid siren sounded. Her father had taught her a little song to sing to herself as she sat in the shelter:

God is our refuge, be not afraid.
He will protect you, all through the raid.
When bombs are falling and danger is near,
He will be with you till the all clear.

It was a comfort to Clara, but at night she still lay awake, imagining German soldiers falling from the sky and marching up Northumberland Street. When she finally fell asleep, her thoughts wove themselves into nightmares.

The Greens never used the brick-built street shelters, which looked so much flimsier than the solid, dark-stone Northumberland Buildings. Since their flat was on the ground floor, Mr Green believed they would be relatively safe in the event of a bomb hitting the roof. Their upstairs neighbours got in the habit of trooping down to join them whenever the siren sounded.

Mrs Green always tried to put the younger children to bed as early as possible, hoping that they would sleep through the raids, although the ever-sociable Rose, now eight, usually snuck out to join the crowd in the living room.

From August 1940 to April 1941, Liverpool suffered nearly seventy air raids, including five major ones, resulting in more than 2,000 fatalities. But the following month, that death toll was matched in just nine days, as the city was pummelled in the May Blitz.

The month started with a relatively light raid, in which the roof of Lime Street Station was damaged and twelve members of the Women's Voluntary Service were killed when an emergency rest centre was hit. The next night's raid was twice as heavy, causing major damage along the docks and in the Castle Street area, gutting the Corn Exchange, and hitting the overhead railway and James Street Station.

It was followed, on 3 May, by Liverpool's worst night of the entire war. For more than six hours, 300 German aircraft dropped 50,000 incendiaries and more than 360 tons of high explosives, causing unprecedented destruction and loss of life. The main shopping area on Lord Street and South John Street was reduced to rubble and the iconic Lewis's department store was gutted. In the 'cultural quarter', the William Brown Library and Museum was extensively damaged, leading to the loss of 150,000 books, as was the Walker Art Gallery. Fires at the India Buildings on Water Street claimed all the Tax Office's records, while the Central Post Office was put out of action. Two more wings of Walton Gaol were destroyed and several hospitals were hit, with the worst incident occurring at Mill Road, where more than eighty people were killed in the hospital itself and fourteen in the ambulance depot, including many mothers and babies. Masonry collapsed on the operating theatre in the basement, where a procedure was already under way. A nurse and two medical students were killed, along with the deputy medical superintendent, while the anaesthetist lost an eye in the attack. The patient was pulled out of the debris and the operation finished successfully at Walton Hospital.

The raid the following night was lighter, since the Luft-waffe was focused on Belfast, but 57 tons of high explosives were dropped across Merseyside, and 34 tons the night after. St Luke's Church was hit, its stained-glass windows destroyed and its bells sent crashing to the ground. A shorter raid on 6 May hit Oxford Street Hospital and the Pier Head, as well as causing damage to the Mill Street area.

It seemed as if the raids were decreasing, but the night of 7 May was to bring an onslaught almost as fierce as that of the 3rd. More than 160 enemy aircraft flew over the city in waves, dropping 30,000 incendiaries and 232 tons of high explosives.

That night Clara, now six, and her ten-year-old brother, Billy, were asleep in their bedroom when they were woken suddenly by a loud crashing noise. Opening her eyes in the darkness, Clara tried to work out what had happened. The air felt dusty, and there was something heavy resting on top of her blanket. When she wriggled her legs, it made a clinking sound, and she realised her bed was covered in glass. Turning her head, she saw that the bedroom window had been blown in.

'Billy!' she cried. 'There's glass all over me bed!'

'We've been bombed,' replied her brother pragmati-cally. 'I suppose we'd better get up.'

Clara peeled the blanket off carefully and climbed out of bed. The two children picked their way across the room in their bare feet, doing their best to avoid the shattered glass that lay strewn all over the floor.

The bedroom door had been blown off its hinges and was lying on its side across the doorway. With Billy's help, Clara climbed over it and out into the corridor, which was full of rubble. Dust caught in her throat and made her cough, and she began to feel afraid. Where were her parents and her sisters? Why were she and Billy all alone?

In the gloom she thought she could see a flashing light and became disorientated. She tripped, and Billy steadied her.

'Come here!' a voice called, but it wasn't one she recognised. The two children stumbled towards it, clambering over piles of rubble into the living room. Outside the window was a fireman with a torch.

'Come to me,' the man said urgently.

Clara and Billy scrambled over furniture and fallen masonry towards the shattered window. Large, strong hands lifted her out of the ruins of the family home. Billy followed moments later.

Black with dirt and dust, the two children were wrapped in blankets and taken to a nearby police station, where they were told to sit on a bench underneath a coat rack.

'You'll be all right now,' the fireman said. 'Just stay there.' Then he rushed off to resume his duties. No one explained to Clara and Billy what had become of the rest of their family.

Clara was just happy that her older brother was there with her. She busied herself with investigating the pockets of the coats hung up behind her, trying to guess what might be inside each of them. After a while a policeman brought them both a steaming mug of cocoa. Then they were left alone again, wondering what was going on.

It wasn't until the following day that the children learned the full story of what had happened. Their father had decided to go to bed early that night, taking little Winnie with him. Mary and Rose had been with their mother and the neighbours in the living room, gathered around the fire chatting, when a parachute bomb floated down. It landed not on the roof of the building but at basement level, exploding upwards directly beneath their flat and the one next door.

The two older girls had found themselves plunged into total darkness, and all the sound seemed to have been drained out of the room. Their ears felt as if they were going to burst, and it was several minutes before they regained enough hearing to notice a low moaning sound. Suddenly, there were flashlights penetrating the gloom and the girls could make out men's voices calling them. When the beam of one of the torches lit up their father's face, they saw blood trickling down his neck and Mary screamed in fear.

She and Rose managed to climb out of the shattered window, Rose cutting her foot badly in the process. Little Winnie followed, but Mr Green refused to leave, insisting on finding his pregnant wife first. As the girls were carried away to safety, all they could hear was their father calling desperately for their mother.

In the confusion that followed the raid, the children became scattered. Rose and Winnie were taken to a neighbouring house, while Mary ended up at a first-aid post. The neighbours who had gathered around the fire with them were taken to hospital with minor injuries but none of them was badly hurt.

Only Mrs Green remained unaccounted for, buried somewhere beneath the rubble. Despite his own injuries, Mr Green worked tirelessly with the rescue workers, determined to dig out his beloved wife, dead or alive.

Mary, sitting in the first-aid post, heard snippets of information from the ARP and Civil Defence workers as they came in and out. At least eight people who had been in the flat next door to the Greens' had died, including the mother of a young soldier who had just come home on leave. The boy had lost his leg and been taken to hospital, where he would die two days later. Two other women were still missing – their scattered body parts would be found on a nearby rooftop a fortnight after the raid.

Elsewhere in the city, more than 300 incidents had been reported, with north Liverpool and Bootle suffering the worst of the devastation. As casualties flooded into Bootle General, incendiaries and high explosives came raining down on the hospital and it had to be evacuated. Bootle ARP Headquarters were destroyed, and the temporary mortuary in Marsh Lane Baths, containing 180 bodies, was engulfed by fire. In the worst incident of the night, a shelter beneath the Co-op on Stanley Road collapsed, killing thirty people in one fell swoop.

*

By daybreak, there was still no news of Mrs Green, heavily pregnant and missing beneath what was left of her former home. The rescue workers had carried on digging all through the night and were utterly exhausted.

Finally, Mr Green managed to find his beloved wife and pull her out of the debris. She was alive but badly injured, with severe bruising and several broken ribs. Mr Green clutched her tenderly, beside himself with relief. Mrs Green would live but there was no knowing what might have happened to the baby.

There were no ambulances available to take her to hospital that morning, so Mr Green left his wife in the care of a neighbour while he tried to locate the rest of the family. He ran around frantically, asking everybody if they had seen his children, but the morning after the raid the entire neighbourhood was in chaos and nobody seemed to know where they had been taken.

Mary was located first and told the good news that her mother had been rescued. Next, Mr Green found Clara and Billy, still sitting on their bench in the police station. He hugged the two of them in relief. Telling them to stay put, he rounded up Rose and Winnie and then returned to collect Mrs Green. It wasn't until noon that all seven of them were reunited, covered in dust and dirt from head to toe and still in their nightclothes but happy beyond words just to be together again.

The Greens were taken in a police car to a rest centre in a church on High Park Street, where other bombed-out families were huddling together on mattresses on the floor.

A doctor tended to Mrs Green's wounds, while Red Cross workers sorted them all out with fresh clothes to wear. Unfortunately, the water supply had been cut off in the raid, so there was no way for them to wash, and they had to put the clean clothes on over their grimy skin.

After a few hours, one of Mr Green's sisters turned up at the rest centre offering to help. Auntie Clara was known as dad's 'posh' sister, since she had married a teacher and lived in a nice house in the small town of Maghull, to the north of Liverpool. She agreed to take in as many of the family as she could, assuring the doctor that she would take good care of her pregnant sister-in-law.

But even the well-off Auntie Clara couldn't accommodate all seven of the Greens alongside her own family. Fortunately, Mr Green's other sister, Auntie Sarah, offered to take the rest of them to her home in Fazakerley, five miles away from Maghull.

The last thing Mr Green wanted was to split up his little family once again, especially with his wife in a delicate condition. But in the circumstances, it was clear he had no choice. He agreed to take Clara, Billy and Rose with him to Fazakerley, while his wife, Winnie and Mary would go to Maghull.

The Greens made a pitiful sight as they traipsed into town to catch the bus out to north Liverpool. It was a long walk, with several detours thanks to unexploded bombs along the way. Poor Mrs Green was in terrible pain, although she never complained.

When they finally arrived at the bus stop, they found a

long queue of people already waiting. But at the sight of their blackened faces, everyone else moved aside, letting them jump to the front of the queue.

Clara and her siblings boarded a bus with their father and Auntie Sarah, waving their mother and sisters good-bye as it drove off. The family had been separated again, and this time there was no knowing how long for.

In Maghull, Mrs Green's broken ribs were strapped up by a doctor, and she, Winnie and Mary were at last able to have a good wash. That evening, they sat and watched the sky turn red again as Liverpool suffered the last and most ferocious of the week's raids. The street behind Northumberland Buildings was among those hit; a fourteen-year-old girl that Mary had been at school with, along with her whole family, were killed.

Meanwhile, in Fazakerley, Auntie Sarah and Uncle Andy were doing their best to make room for their unexpected guests, but the only place they could find for Rose and Clara to sleep was a walk-in wardrobe. Auntie Sarah moved out her clothes and laid a mattress down on the floor, and the girls did their best to adjust to their cramped new bedroom.

Clara's father assured her it would only be temporary and that the council would rehouse them soon. In the weeks that followed, Mr Green frequently went down to the council offices to enquire whether they had found his family a new home, but every time they sent him away again with the answer that nothing had come up yet.

He also made regular trips to Maghull to see his wife, who was rapidly approaching her due date. True to her word, Auntie Clara was taking good care of Mrs Green, as well as taking four-year-old Winnie in hand. Since the death of little Betty, Winnie was the baby of the family once again and was used to being mollycoddled by her parents. But Auntie Clara wouldn't stand for spoilt children. Whenever Winnie threatened to throw a tantrum because she didn't get her way, her aunt would fill up a jug with cold water and pour it over the little girl's head.

Over in Fazakerley, Clara, Rose and Billy rarely got to see their mother now, and they missed her terribly. Having their cousins Dennis, Kevin, Eddie and Marie around to play with proved a useful distraction, especially as they had not been able to go to school since being bombed out. Clara had only just learned to read at St Pat's and, keen to encourage her, Mr Green brought her as many books as he could lay his hands on.

At last, Mr Green's constant hassling of the council paid off and they were assigned a new house. He was over the moon at the thought of finally being able to get his family back together again and rushed over to pick up the keys straight after work.

He made his way to the address he had been given, to check that the property was suitable. When he reached the street, he walked along counting the door numbers until he arrived at the correct one. But instead of a house, all he could see was a mountain of rubble, and the door to which he held the key lay broken on top of the pile.

Bitterly disappointed, Mr Green returned to the council offices. 'You've handed me the keys to a bombsite!' he told the man there.

'Sorry,' the council officer shrugged. 'Our records got destroyed in the raids, so we don't know which houses are still standing. We'll let you know when another one comes up.'

Mr Green traipsed back to north Liverpool to break the bad news to his family. He knew his wife would be disappointed not to be in her own home by the time she gave birth, especially since, given the injuries she had sustained in the bombing, there was no knowing what complications there might be.

In the event, it was a long and painful labour, much more so than any of Mrs Green's previous six pregnancies. But on 1 July 1941, she delivered a healthy little boy, whom she named Tony. He was a big, bouncing baby, with the loudest cry of any of the Green children.

Mr Green was soon hounding the council again, demanding that they give the family priority since they had been split up for two months now and they had six homeless children to look after.

After waiting another long month, he received the good news that a second house had become available. He made his way to the new address, the keys clutched in readiness. But as he approached the correct door number, he couldn't believe his eyes. Once again, the promised home was nothing more than a pile of bricks.

Mr Green was a patient man by nature, but even he was beginning to lose his cool. Back he went to the council, demanding that this time they find him place to live that included such basic amenities as walls and a roof.

Another month went by, and then another. By now young Mary was old enough to go out to work, so she joined her Maghull cousins, Molly and Betty, at the Enca factory in Aintree, making yarn for the inner tyres of aircraft. Like her, they were talented musicians, and Molly in particular was an excellent pianist. So much so that they were called on to play for the rest of the workers, as well as the millions of listeners tuning in all over the country, when the morale-boosting BBC radio programme *Workers' Playtime* visited their factory canteen.

Time was passing, and the Greens had been living as two separate families for five months now. Mr Green was missing out on seeing baby Tony growing bigger and learning to crawl. Meanwhile, Clara and her siblings had missed out on nearly half a year of school. For Billy in particular, the timing couldn't have been worse. He lost the chance to sit the scholarship exam, and with it the possibility of going to grammar school. A shy but intelligent child, he might have blossomed in a selective environment, but now he would never have that opportunity.

Mr Green had hoped to get a decent-sized house for his growing family, but the separation from his beloved wife and the break-up of their family was becoming unbearable. The next time he visited the council offices, he begged the clerk to see if there was anything available, no matter how small.

'Would you take a tenement flat?' the man asked him. 'There's one going in Myrtle Gardens.'

The vast tenement blocks were a familiar sight in Liverpool, especially in former slum areas that had been cleared in the 1930s. Myrtle Gardens was in Edge Hill, an area of the city where the Greens didn't know a soul, but Mr Green was in no position to be picky.

'I'll take anything to get my family back together,' he replied. He just hoped that this time the building wouldn't turn out to have already been bombed.

As it happened, the corner flat the Greens had been assigned was one of several in the block that had been taken out by a bomb earlier in the war. In one of them, a whole family had been wiped out by the blast, and the explosion had also killed two men on a nearby anti-aircraft gun as well as a stray dog that happened to be passing. A child emerging from an air-raid shelter later found the dog hanging from some railings with its guts blown out and had suffered nightmares for weeks afterwards as a result.

But the damaged flats had since been rebuilt, and now they were the best in the block. After satisfying himself that their new home was indeed still standing, Mr Green broke the happy news to the rest of the family.

At last, after more than five months' separation, the Greens were reunited. Clara could see her mother's body physically relax at the relief of being back with her husband.

For her own part, she was happy to have a bedroom to sleep in again rather than a wardrobe.

In fact, the new flat in Myrtle Gardens turned out to have not two but three bedrooms, so the boys and girls could sleep separately for the first time. It also boasted an indoor bathroom with the luxury of both hot and cold running water, while outside there were two separate playgrounds for the children.

With more than 300 flats, the enormous block seemed imposing to begin with. Mrs Green in particular missed the support of family, as well as the friends and neighbours they had known in Toxteth. But despite its size, the tenement had a strong sense of community, and it soon began to feel like home.

Not long afterwards, the Greens were blessed with their eighth and final child, a little boy called John, who completed their family and their happiness.

12

CHRISTOPHER

'Suffering Jesus!' cried Mrs Munro, crossing herself as a German plane thundered overhead.

She began to pray under her breath while her three children, John, Rita and Christopher, huddled in terror beneath their coats on the cold cellar floor.

A bomb exploded somewhere nearby, causing the cellar walls to shake violently. Instinctively, Mrs Munro threw herself over her children to protect them.

The Munros lived in cramped Victorian 'court' housing on Silvester Street, a hundred yards from the River Mersey. They knew that at any minute one of the bombs intended for the Liverpool docks could miss its target and flatten their little house instead.

Their next-door neighbours had already suffered that fate, as had the next house along. Since the on-street shelters were always full, they just had to take their chances in the cellar, hoping that they wouldn't be next.

Mrs Munro had wanted her children to be evacuated to Wales like the other local kids, but her husband, a merchant seaman, had refused to let them go and live with strangers. At two and a half, Christopher had grown used to falling asleep to the sound of bombs ever since the Liverpool Blitz had started eight months earlier. By now he was almost oblivious to it.

The last few evenings, however, had been different. It was the fourth night of the May Blitz and their neighbourhood of Scotland Road, to the north of Liverpool city centre, was getting a particularly bad hammering. By the time the all clear sounded the following morning, parts of it would be unrecognisable.

A few minutes' walk away up Scottie Road, the famous Rotunda Theatre was already engulfed in flames. By 2 a.m., the building had collapsed in on itself, destroying both the theatre and the pub underneath.

On nearby Athol Street, the gasworks suffered a direct hit, destroying one of the gasometers, while Hadfield's bone fertiliser works was badly damaged, sending foul-smelling fumes into the air.

By 4.30 a.m., when the German planes finally turned back, 11,563 incendiaries and 57 tons of high explosives had been dropped on Merseyside.

That morning, the Munros crept out of the cellar and went to see what was left of their local area. Police, fire and demolition teams had been working through the night trying to clear debris and pull out survivors, and many of them were still at work. Huge pipes ran along the gutters, supplying water to the firefighters, and everything was a mass of smoke and rubble. As they reached Athol Street, Christopher stared in confusion at the once-familiar area, which was now flat as a pancake.

It was Monday morning, but there would be no school for John and Rita, since St Silvester's infant and junior schools had also been bombed overnight – luckily, without any casualties. On the Saturday night, twenty-four people had died sheltering in the basement of another local school on Addison Street, when it was hit by a parachute mine.

Yet amidst all this destruction, the traditional Scouse humour was still evident. Signs had been put up on several comprehensively bombed-out shops that read simply, 'Business as usual'.

For the local children, the air raids had reshaped the urban landscape, creating areas of wasteland that could be claimed as unofficial playgrounds. The patch of Silvester Street where the neighbours' houses had once stood was known in the local slang as the 'ollah' and had become the kids' favourite hangout.

Unfortunately, the ollah also provided easy access to the entryway behind the Munros' house, which soon became a favoured spot for amorous couples. Little Christopher often wondered what the grunts and groans were that he heard coming from the alleyway when he played there.

He had heard similar noises coming from his parents' bedroom whenever his father was back on dry land after a long spell at sea. When Mr Munro returned to Liverpool, the first thing he did was take his wife upstairs for a few hours while the children waited patiently down below.

'What are they doing up there?' Christopher asked his older sister one time.

'It's the birds and the bees,' Rita replied vaguely.

Mr Munro always came home from sea in a good mood, and with a wallet stuffed full of cash from all the overtime he had accrued on his voyage. Everyone in Scottie Road knew it, and he couldn't walk past a pub without one of his 'friends' calling him in for a drink, which Mr Munro invariably paid for. Anyone with money troubles would tap him up, knowing that he was a soft touch.

Before he knew it, all the money he'd earned at sea would have disappeared and Mr Munro would have to sign on to another ship. Often he was gone for six months or more, during which time the rest of the family would lurch from feast to famine. At such times, tea for the Munros consisted of just a piece of bread and jam.

While her husband was away, Christopher's mum would make some extra money busking in the local pubs, singing and playing piano box for the appreciative dockers. With her jet-black hair and Irish good looks, Mrs Munro could still turn a few heads. She never told Mr Munro about it when he came back, knowing that he wouldn't approve.

At times, things got so bad that she had to visit the local moneylender or pawn anything she could, even the bedclothes, just to make ends meet. But whatever the state of the family's finances, she never failed to leave a shilling on the mantlepiece for the parish priest, Father McNamara, who would call round every Friday to collect it.

*

All week, the kids looked forward to Saturday mornings, when they got a free cup of cocoa and a bun at the Lee Jones League of Wellwishers club on Silvester Street. But their greatest treat came once a month, when Mrs Munro received her allotment of wages from their father's shipping company. She would always take them down to Thorn's cafe on Scottie Road for a proper roast dinner, followed by suet pudding and custard.

One day, Christopher and his family were on their way to Thorn's when a German plane suddenly appeared in the sky above their heads, and then – to their horror – swooped down low.

'Run!' shouted Christopher's mother, grabbing him by the hand and dragging him, stumbling, into the doorway of the nearest shop. John and Rita followed close behind.

The four of them stood cowering inside, as the plane flew up Scotland Road, strafing the local market as it went. Not long afterwards, the pilot lost control of the aircraft and it dropped like a stone into the Mersey, much to the excitement of the local kids, who rushed down to witness the spectacle.

The Munro children, however, were not among their number. Once the coast was clear, they had emerged from the shop and headed straight to Thorn's, where they were now busily tucking into their roast dinner. Their monthly treat was a hallowed tradition and not even being machine-gunned by a German plane could keep them from it.

*

Once the May Blitz had passed, the worst was over for the people of Liverpool. For the rest of the year the city experienced just a few minor raids, with the last bombs falling on 10 January 1942 in Toxteth. But in the Munro household, the war was never far away. Christopher's father had been at sea since November on a steamship called the *Empress of Asia*, which had been requisitioned by the Admiralty to carry troops and supplies to Africa, India and Singapore.

One day in February 1942 there was a knock on the door. Mrs Munro opened it to find a telegram boy waiting outside in his smart black uniform and gleaming cap.

Every wartime housewife dreaded the appearance of the telegram boys, known colloquially as 'angels of death' since they often came bearing the worst news. Little more than children themselves, they were ill-equipped to deal with the emotional impact of the messages they brought, which often saw women screaming, fainting or bursting into tears while the awkward teenager waited on their doorstep.

Mrs Munro had cried her eyes out when one of their neighbours had received a similar visit and learned that her husband – the father of one of Christopher's friends – had been killed in action. Now, the lad on her own door-step was handing her a telegram too.

Fearing the worst, she ripped open the envelope with shaking hands. Inside, she found a note from the merchant navy explaining that her husband was missing in action. 'Suffering Jesus,' sobbed Mrs Munro.

It would be some time before the family learned the full story. A few days earlier, as the *Empress* approached Singapore, Christopher's father had been shovelling coal in the engine room when the ship was dive-bombed by nine Japanese planes. An Australian vessel, the HMAS *Yarra*, had been escorting the convoy and managed to shoot down one of the enemy aircraft and damage several others. It then manoeuvred its bow alongside the stern of the burning steamship and rescued 1,804 men. Another vessel, the HMAS *Bendigo*, saved seventy-eight more. The last two people off the boat were the captain and chief engineer, who were picked up by the HMAS *Wollongong* just as the ship sank. But sixteen men died in the attack, and all the military equipment and supplies the *Empress* had been carrying were lost. Ten days later, Singapore fell to the Japanese.

On the wireless, Mrs Munro listened to Nazi propagandist Lord Haw-Haw crowing that the whereabouts of the *Empress* were unknown. Its wreck would not be found for another sixty-eight years.

But Mrs Munro was concerned only for her husband, and missing in action wasn't the same as dead. The family waited anxiously for the telegram boy to knock again. When he finally did, Christopher's mother went to the door and once again took the missive with shaking hands.

Christopher and his siblings braced themselves as their mother scanned the words of the telegram. Those few seconds seemed to last an eternity.

Then she turned to them. 'He's alive!' she cried. 'Thank God, he's alive!'

She ran over to the children, grabbing their hands and dancing around the room with joy, much to the embarrassment of the young telegram boy.

Sure enough, Mr Munro soon returned to Silvester Street, but he was not in a good way. Down in the engine room, he had been safe from the initial dive-bombing, but he'd inhaled toxic fumes and been hospitalised with emphysema. Now he coughed and spluttered constantly and struggled to get his breath.

But the merchant navy wasn't done with Mr Munro yet. Sailors were exempt from conscription as long as they signed an agreement to carry on working, but when they did so, many of them had no idea how perilous the job would become. In the first two years of the war alone, almost half of all British merchant seamen were reported dead or missing. Unsurprisingly, plenty of them jumped ship in America or Australia, or went AWOL once they got home.

Christopher had seen military police knocking on doors to arrest deserters before, but he was shocked when they turned up at the house on Silvester Street one day, asking for his father.

'Don't worry, it's all a mistake,' Mr Munro told his family. 'I just need to show them my discharge papers.'

He and his wife began searching the house, while the policemen looked on impatiently. But try as they might, they couldn't find them.

'Right then, you're coming with us,' one of the men said, grabbing Mr Munro by the arm.

'No, no please!' Mrs Munro begged, clinging to her husband. 'He's not a deserter!'

But the military police clearly didn't believe them. Mr Munro was arrested and taken down to St Anne Street Police Station.

Christopher watched helplessly as his mother began to sob. Having only just got her husband back from a sinking ship, this latest separation was more than she could bear.

With the help of the children, she searched the house from top to bottom, until eventually they found the discharge papers. Then she raced down to the police station clutching them in her hand. Not long afterwards, her husband was allowed to come home again.

Christopher was relieved to have his father back, but the question remained of how the misunderstanding had occurred in the first place. Someone must have reported Mr Munro to the police, and there was a suspicion that Mrs Munro's parents might have had something to do with it. There had long been resentment between the Bowmans and the Munros, and Christopher's grandmother, in particular, had never had much time for her son-in-law.

In fact, no one on Mum's side of the family seemed to like Christopher very much either, perhaps because he took after the fair-haired Scottish Munros more than he did the Irish Bowmans. With his dad away at sea so much of the time, Christopher often felt like the black sheep of the family, absorbing the unspoken resentment that had previously been directed at his father.

Even Christopher's own mother wasn't immune to such prejudices. She made no secret of the fact that she favoured Christopher's elder brother, John, who was treated as the golden child of the family. Christopher, meanwhile, was her scapegoat and got the blame for everything that went wrong.

It was only when Dad was around that Christopher felt there was someone in his corner. As a result, whenever his father went away to sea he would feel a cloud of sadness descending on him.

It was Dad who stood up for Christopher when John played a particularly nasty trick on him. Christopher had followed his older brother down to 'the Cut', the section of the Leeds and Liverpool Canal where all the local boys swam. Mr Munro had learned to swim there himself as a boy, and now John had followed in his footsteps, becoming a strong swimmer.

Christopher was yet to follow suit, and John decided to take it upon himself to teach his younger brother to swim the hard way. He snuck up behind Christopher as he stood at the water's edge and gave him a shove.

Before he realised what was happening, Christopher found himself underwater. He sank down a few feet, flailing wildly in an attempt to get back to the surface. As he did so, his foot became caught on a piece of twisted metal – the remains of an old pram or a rusty bike that had sunk to the bottom of the canal. Christopher thrashed and thrashed but no matter how hard he tried, he couldn't free himself.

Christopher's lungs felt as if they were bursting and he was convinced he was about to die. He would almost certainly have drowned if a local docker, Jimmy Clarke, hadn't jumped in after him.

Jimmy had arrived in Liverpool four decades earlier as a stowaway on a ship from British Guiana and had since become something of a local legend. He was an excellent swimmer and had already saved several young children from drowning in the Leeds and Liverpool Canal, leading to the local motto: 'If you can't see Jim, don't dip in.'

Now it was Christopher's turn to be rescued by Scotland Road's favourite have-a-go hero. Jimmy dived under the water and pulled him free from the rusty metal, bringing him back up to the surface coughing and spluttering.

Christopher's young life might have just flashed in front of his eyes, but before long it was his brother, John, who was in a state of abject terror. Unlike most fathers in the area, Mr Munro never took his belt to his kids, but when he heard what John had done to Christopher, he made an exception, pulling his older son's trousers down, putting him over his knee and giving him the thrashing of his life.

Christopher listened to his brother's screams with satisfaction, knowing that for once there was nothing their mother could do to help him.

Unfortunately, it wasn't long before Mr Munro took a job on another ship, despite his ill health.

'Why do you keep going away to sea?' Christopher asked him sadly.

'Who'd feed you lot if I didn't?' his father replied.

Although Mrs Munro had got herself a job at the nearby Tate & Lyle factory, packing little boxes of demerara sugar, what she earned there would never be enough to keep a family of five.

Soon Dad was gone again, and before long money was as tight as before. Mum's rings and clothes went back to the pawnshop, as did the family's bedclothes, so they all slept under piles of coats instead.

By now, Christopher had started school, and the hot dinners there meant he got at least one good meal a day. As a result, his attendance was exemplary, despite the fact that he was always at the bottom of the class, spending most of his time daydreaming about ways he could make money for his family rather than concentrating on what the teachers were saying.

Christopher was an enterprising boy and was already monetising his talents. He had discovered he was an expert thrower and could thrash the other kids when they played 'nearest the wall' with bottle tops. When he had won enough tops to fill a jam jar he would take them down to Thomas's scrap yard and sell them for a bit of cash.

Next he moved on to selling aluminium tins, which he scavenged from neighbours' bins in the entryway. The local housewives didn't seem to mind when they saw him climbing on the wall. Some of them even gave him their old rags to offer to the rag-and-bone man as well, though more often than not what he got for these was not cash but a balloon or a goldfish in a jar.

Soon, though, Christopher had set his sights on more lucrative activities. His partner in crime was Pat Burke, who also lived in the courts and was known to everyone as 'Spam', since he was rarely seen without a spam butty in his hand.

On Sunday mornings, the boys would sneak into the local bombed-out houses and break up the old wooden floorboards for firewood, which they tied up into little bundles and sold door-to-door for a penny a pop. At Cazneau Street Market, they would ask the stallholders for their empty orange crates at the end of the day, which could also be broken up and sold as kindling.

For the most part, Mrs Munro was more than happy to receive a cut of Christopher's earnings from his latest business venture, but there was one scheme she didn't approve of. He and some older boys had begun following Tate & Lyle's open-top wagons down to the Dock Road half a mile away, where they were loaded up with bags of raw sugar that had come from the Caribbean. Climbing up the sides of the vehicles, the boys would slash the bags with a razor and catch the sugar in the fold of their jumpers as it spilled out, then jump back down and take it home to boil up into toffee.

When Christopher's mother discovered he was robbing her employer, she was determined to put a stop to it, and she soon came up with an effective solution.

'You know cockroaches lay their eggs in raw sugar?' she told her son casually one day.

'Really?' replied Christopher, horrified.

'Oh yeah,' Mrs Munro continued. 'And they can breed a hundred-fold every twenty-four hours.'

Christopher lay awake all that night, terrified that cockroach eggs were hatching inside his stomach, and he vowed never to steal sugar again.

His next scheme, however, was even more audacious. He and his mates had begun pinching corn from the J. Bibby & Sons grain warehouse and selling it on to local pigeon fanciers. After a while, though, they realised they could put it to much better use. On Sunday mornings, when the local factories were all closed, they would climb the thirteen storeys to the roof of a tobacco warehouse on Regent Road, lay a trail of corn leading up to a little wall, and then crouch behind it, waiting for a pigeon to land.

After a while, a hungry bird would begin pecking at the corn, following the trail until it led them right up to the wall. Then one of the boys would leap over, pounce on the hapless bird and wring its neck.

Once they had collected half a dozen pigeons this way, they would descend to ground level again, with the birds stuffed inside their jumpers. Often, the most recent catches were still flapping about in their death throes.

The boys would then tour the local cafes selling their quarry for sixpence each, to be turned into that afternoon's pigeon pie.

After repeating this routine three or four times in a morning, Christopher and his friends ended up with a decent amount of money in their pockets. They would go home for a bite to eat and then meet up again later for a game of cards, gambling with the money they had made on the birds. Christopher was a skilled card player and usually won, so by the time he went home for tea, his pockets were bulging with cash. Mrs Munro got about ten bob from him most weeks, although unfortunately John soon began demanding a cut of the takings as well, threatening to beat his little brother up – like a Mafia enforcer running a protection scam.

As time went on, Christopher and his friends expanded the scope of their operations. Despite his mother's protestations, they began stealing brown sugar from the Tate & Lyle refinery, which they bagged up and sold door-to-door, as well as exchanging clothing coupons, food coupons and ration packs for cash or Woodbine cigarettes. Christopher would then gamble with his earnings, playing pitch and toss or dice with grown men in the alleyways and frequently turning a tidy profit.

But in the close-knit community of Scottie Road, his behaviour didn't go unnoticed for long. Soon news of what Christopher was getting up to reached his mother's ears. With her husband away at sea, she turned to the local priest for help with her wayward son.

Father McNamara duly turned up to give six-year-old Christopher a stern talking-to, lecturing him about how good Catholic boys ought to behave. But Christopher had little respect for the priest, having witnessed him taking his shilling from the mantlepiece each week, even when the family was practically starving. He looked Father McNamara straight in the eye and told him where to stick his advice, making use of every four-letter word in his vocabulary.

Mrs Munro was horrified and began apologising profusely, while Father McNamara's face turned red with fury. But Christopher was unrepentant. He legged it before his mother could start haranguing him as well, but his refusal to bow to the priest's authority made his relationship with her more strained than ever.

Christopher knew his mother was deeply embarrassed by his misdeeds, worried about him sullying the family's good name. But the way he saw it, he was entitled to shift for himself. Even as a child, he had seen how money could transform a person's life. He and his friends sometimes lurked around the entrance to the fancy Adelphi Hotel near Lime Street Station, asking the wealthy guests for spare change as they emerged from the elegant revolving doors. Seeing these people enjoying a life of luxury, little more than a mile from the slums of Silvester Street, had been an eye-opener.

Like many boys in the war years, Christopher was growing up without much input from his father. During the brief periods when Mr Munro was at home, his wife would tell him all about what his boys had been up to in his absence, praising John's behaviour while lamenting Christopher's, in the hope that he might enact some rough discipline. The more he heard of his mother's damning reports, the more Christopher's resentment grew. One day, when she announced that she'd recently caught him smoking, he responded by swearing to her face.

This, at least, certainly got Mr Munro's attention. Christopher had never seen his dad look so angry before, and rather than wait to learn his punishment, he bolted out of the house, not even stopping to put his shoes on. Mr Munro soon gave chase.

Christopher did his best to lose his father amongst the streets and alleyways of industrial Liverpool. But when he ran through a muddy puddle, he felt something sharp underfoot, followed by a searing pain that stopped him in his tracks.

Christopher lifted his foot out of the water and saw that it was dripping with blood. A piece of broken glass had made a three-inch gash in it.

Unable to run any further, Christopher had no choice but to wait for his father to catch up with him. But at the sight of his son barefoot and bleeding, the angry look on Mr Munro's face changed to one of concern. He took off his shirt and wrapped it tenderly around his son's injury. 'Why can't you just do what you're told?' he sighed, shaking his head as he pressed down hard to stop the bleeding. Then he lifted Christopher into his arms and carried him almost a mile to the Northern Hospital.

There, Christopher's wound was soon cleaned and stitched up, but he remained in hospital for two days so the doctors could check it wasn't infected.

When he did finally get home, he received no sympathy from his mother. 'It's your own fault,' was all she had to say to him.

Christopher couldn't help thinking that if it had been John who was wounded, her reaction would have been very different.

After the war, Mr Munro decided his family needed a fresh start, so they moved to the leafy suburb of Croxteth, on the outskirts of the city. But the more salubrious environment did nothing to improve Christopher's behaviour when his father was away at sea. By the age of ten, he had been arrested for stealing apples from a nearby farm, and since his mother refused to pay the fine, he was taken to the notorious Woolton Vale Remand Home to serve a ten-day sentence. There, he was beaten so badly that he fell over and ended up in hospital with concussion. But when he got home, Mrs Munro's only comment upon seeing him again was, 'That'll teach you a lesson.'

The experience in the remand home did nothing to curb Christopher's lawless tendencies. By the age of seventeen, he was robbing upmarket clothes shops and jewellers, until eventually he was caught by the police with thousands of pounds' worth of furs.

Christopher spent more than two years in a borstal, but it turned out to be the making of him. While there, he finally got the education he had missed out on at school. He came out determined to turn his life around.

13

JOHN

After London, the Luftwaffe's blitz on Liverpool was the worst of the war, turning the lives of tens of thousands of children upside down. Among them was nine-year-old John Le Page, who had never even been to the city. John was living sixty miles away in Halifax at the time, but his real home was much further away: the British Crown Dependency of Guernsey.

John's family had fled to England a year earlier, just days before the Germans arrived to occupy the Channel Islands. He and his little sister Betty were among more than 5,000 Guernsey children now living as refugees on the mainland.

Many of the kids had waved farewell to their parents not knowing that they wouldn't see them again for five years. John and Betty, however, were more fortunate: their mum and dad had decided to evacuate with them.

Mr Le Page, a grower of tomatoes and flowers for export, had shut up his greenhouses and gone round their home on the northern tip of the island, carefully boarding up all the windows. The family's furniture had been sent to a warehouse in town, and precious belongings such as silverware entrusted to John's Aunt Elsa and Uncle Jack, who had decided to stay for the duration of the war.

On the morning of 28 June 1940, the Le Pages arrived at the harbour in Guernsey's capital, St Peter Port. Their boat was the second to last out before the Germans arrived, and the crossing was a rough one, spent sitting on top of the cargo hold in the open air.

After a miserable six-hour voyage, John and his family arrived in Weymouth, on the Dorset coast, but they weren't allowed to disembark right away. Instead, they had to remain at sea for several hours, waiting for permission to dock. One of the previous evacuation boats had hit a stray mine and sunk just offshore, so the authorities weren't taking any chances.

At last the boat pulled up to a jetty, and a few minutes later John was relieved to feel cobblestones beneath his feet again.

The Le Pages were ushered into a large hall, along with hundreds of fellow refugees from the Channel Islands, for processing by an army of women sporting the grey-green uniform of the WVS.

'Do you have anywhere to go?' one of the ladies asked them kindly.

'Yes,' John's father replied. 'My wife has a cousin in Newton Abbot.' Most Channel Islanders would be relying on the kindness of strangers in England, but the Le Pages were lucky to have family they could call on.

'Well, in that case, carry on!' the lady replied cheerfully, ushering them towards the door.

It was a fifty-mile journey to the Devon market town, and they arrived, bleary-eyed and exhausted, to find Cousin Hilda's modest house already full to bursting. John's mother wasn't the only Guernsey relative who had thrown themselves on Hilda's mercy. She already had his Aunt Frances staying with her, plus his Uncle Vic and his wife, along with their various children.

That evening, John and Betty had to squeeze into a double bed with no fewer than six of their cousins. The only way they could manage it was to sleep in two rows, with four kids at the top and four at the bottom. They slept fitfully, despite John's best efforts, as the oldest of the bunch, to soothe the younger ones with a repertoire of bedtime stories.

The next morning, much to John's relief, his parents began looking for somewhere else to stay. Fortunately, Mr Le Page found his horticultural skills were in demand, especially with so many young farm labourers having been conscripted. He secured a position with a market gardener in the village of Sowton, just outside Exeter, which came with a beautiful thatched cottage for the family to live in.

For young John, the summer of 1940 was idyllic. He and Betty attended the tiny village school, joining a mixed-age class of just ten other children. They spent their weekends playing in the meadows and munching on juicy red apples from the orchard adjoining their garden. Sometimes the farmer let them take turns riding his horse around one of the fields.

JOHN

John became good friends with the farmer's son, and one day after school they snuck into the farm shop together. There, his friend taught him how to turn the tap on the barrel containing his dad's best scrumpy. John had never tasted alcohol before, and although he wasn't sure he liked the taste, the novelty of the experience was still thrilling.

All in all, the Le Pages were thriving in the Devon countryside, and even worrying news from home wasn't enough to dampen their spirits. With Guernsey now under occupation by German forces, their only communication with those family members who had remained on the island – among them his Aunt Elsa, Uncle Jack and grandmother Florence – was via the Red Cross message service. These short missives, received every six months, would be delivered to a local bureau and then passed on to the evacuees. It was through such brief messages that John learned his grandmother's cat had died and that his cousin Walter had started school.

The Red Cross messages were censored, but islanders were ingenious when it came to outwitting the Germans, employing a variety of code words to communicate illicit information – a 'visit from Mother Hubbard', for example, to indicate they were struggling for food.

One day, John's grandmother sent a message that read simply: MRS LANBURY VERY UNWELL. INTERNAL TROUBLE.

Lanbury was the name of the family home in Vale Parish, and the meaning of the message was clear. While the Le Pages were settling down in rural Devon, German soldiers had taken up residence in their house.

A hundred miles away in England, it was hard to imagine getting up close and personal with the enemy, as John knew his relatives back home must be doing. With thousands of German soldiers now stationed in Guernsey, it would be all but impossible to avoid them.

Some, in fact, were already making friends with local children, offering the kids toys and ice cream. Many German soldiers had left families of their own back home, and treating the local children helped ease the pain of separation. For their part, the islanders were growing used to the complex dance of the occupied, doing their best to maintain cordial relations with their well-behaved but very much unwanted guests.

For John, such compromises were unfathomable, especially once the Luftwaffe began bombing cities up and down the United Kingdom.

In their rural idyll, the Le Pages were pretty safe from the German air raids. After all, Sowton was exactly the sort of place that city kids were evacuated to during the war. Their nearest serious target was Exeter, a good five miles away. The first raid there, less than six weeks after the Le Pages had arrived in the area, had succeeded only in blowing up a few chickens and frightening a canary to death. It wouldn't be until two years later that the city would receive its own proper blitz, as part of the so-called Baedeker raids – named for the German guidebook from which the targets were apparently selected.

But even now, the Le Pages' sleepy Devon village wasn't totally immune from danger. One crisp autumn morning, John rushed out of the front door of the cottage to find a large patch of scorched grass in the front garden. At the centre of it was a piece of green metal, about four inches long – the tail fin of a B1E incendiary bomb that had evidently burned itself out overnight.

'Mum, look what I've found!' John shouted, rushing inside with the tail fin clutched in his hand.

His mother took one look at it and screamed. She couldn't help thinking what might have happened if the bomb had landed a few metres closer, on the thatched roof of the cottage.

A glance outside did little to assuage Mrs Le Page's fears. Down the lane, one of the farmer's hayricks was ablaze, having been caught by another of the German incendiaries during the night.

That evening, Mrs Le Page told her husband she'd made a decision. 'We can't stay here,' she insisted. 'It isn't safe.'

Reluctantly, John, Betty and their father packed their bags once again. This time, nestled safely inside John's luggage was the German tail fin that had prompted his mother's decision to leave.

Soon the family were on their way to Halifax, where another uncle from Guernsey had already settled. There was a large community of islanders in the busy Yorkshire town and Mrs Le Page felt sure they would be safe there.

Unfortunately, she was soon proven wrong. Barely had the Le Pages arrived in Halifax when the sirens began wailing. The family spent their first night there cowering in an air-raid shelter.

'The blighters have followed us up here!' Mrs Le Page cried.

Her husband, meanwhile, was struggling to find gainful employment up north. The family were now living in a basement flat on Union Street, just outside the town centre, and the rent wasn't going to pay itself.

But Mr Le Page wasn't only thinking about money. Since leaving Guernsey, he had been nursing a desire to do something meaningful for the war effort. His wife's brothers were both serving in the forces already, Alf in the army and Eddie in the air force. Mr Le Page's health had precluded him from signing up as well, since he had suffered bronchial problems since childhood. He did, however, find another organisation that would have him – one that had come into its own as the German bombing campaign against England began: the Auxiliary Fire Service (AFS).

Established under the Air Raid Precautions Act of 1937, the AFS was a kind of sister service to the much larger ARP. Every city at risk from German bombing had its own auxiliary fire station, staffed by amateur firemen who had received just sixty hours of basic training but were expected to support the work of the local professionals. John's father was among 200,000 auxiliary firemen now stationed up and down the country.

In his new role, Mr Le Page was in his element. Although he had worked as a grower all his life, he had always been more interested in machines than plants. As a young man, he had loved nothing more than tinkering with the engine of his motorbike, and he had only gone into growing because his father needed someone to take over his greenhouses. Now, John saw his dad's eyes light up as he told him all about the AFS's new trailer pumps, which could be towed behind cars, vans or even requisitioned taxis, reaching blazes that traditional bulky fire engines couldn't get close to.

Mr Le Page was a naturally laid-back man – his nickname in the family was Lumpadaddy – but in his smart black AFS uniform, complete with a gold star on the cap, he seemed to walk just a little bit straighter. The job had given him a newfound sense of pride.

John, too, was making the most of life up north. Compared to both Guernsey and Devon, Halifax was bitingly cold, but as Christmas approached, the nippy weather did bring some consolations. Snow rarely fell in Guernsey but Halifax was blanketed in it, and for a boy of nine there could be little that was more exciting. John was even fascinated by the series of yellow holes in the banked-up snow at the side of the roads, left by the town's canine residents. He had never seen anything like it before.

As in Devon, John wasted no time making friends in Halifax. That Christmas, he visited his new schoolfriend Jeff in the suburb of Boothtown. The boys spent all morning building the biggest snowball they could, gradually rolling it down the centre of the empty road until it was taller than they were. Once the ball was too heavy for them to push any further, they abandoned it for the first hapless driver who came along to deal with.

Mr Le Page's work with the fire service could take him away for days at a time. Often the first thing the family would know about his whereabouts was when a postcard arrived from a town that had recently been bombed. He always carried one, self-addressed, in his uniform pocket, so he could let them know where he had ended up.

Back at home, John's father was the warm-hearted family man of old, and now his days off meant he could actually spend more time with his children than when he had been out in the fields every day. One afternoon, he took John to the local cinema to watch *Pinocchio* in glorious Technicolor. Colour films were still a rarity at the time and the dazzling Disney movie enchanted them both.

As 1941 dawned and the German bombing raids continued up and down the country, John got increasingly used to his father's absences. So when he disappeared for a week at the start of May, the rest of the family weren't particularly worried.

Sure enough, a postcard soon arrived announcing that Mr Le Page was in Liverpool, helping the Merseyside fire crews to tackle the devastating May Blitz.

It was another week before John saw his father again, and when he did he was shocked by the change in him. Mr Le Page was a shadow of his former self. He had lost about three stone in weight and his breathing was shallow and laboured. John had never seen his father look so ill.

John

The next day, Mr Le Page tried to go back to work. He only managed a few hours, before returning home later that morning. A doctor came to see him and immediately summoned an ambulance to take him to Halifax General Hospital. But by the time it arrived, John's father was already dead.

The cause of death was given as bronchial pneumonia, brought on by the fires in Liverpool. He had been just thirty-two years old.

With the whole family reeling from the sudden, tragic loss, young John felt a new weight on his shoulders. At just nine years old, he was the man of the family now, and his mother clearly expected him to step up to the mark. While she and Uncle Vic were busy taking care of the funeral arrangements, handing over £22 8s 6d for a beautiful waxed-elm coffin, John was put in charge of the family's food shopping.

Every night, alone in his room, he lay in bed with a single thought going round in his head: 'Why did it happen?' But he always made sure to put on a brave face when the sun rose the following morning.

A week or so later, John and Betty watched from the front step of the house in Union Street as their father's funeral cortège passed by. The fire service took good care of their own and dozens of officers had turned out in their uniforms to pay their respects. But as the procession moved on towards the graveyard, the children were left at home alone, where they waited for their mother to return.

When she did, Mrs Le Page was in no fit state to look after them. She and her husband had been childhood sweethearts, and she was so traumatised by his sudden death that she was admitted to hospital herself not long afterwards.

For the next few months, John and Betty stayed with the family of another of his schoolfriends, Fred Marshall. The Marshalls had a cottage in Hebden Bridge, on the edge of the Yorkshire Moors, and John spent his days outside, wandering the wild, windswept landscape. One day, he made it all the way to Ilkley, a good eighteen miles away.

Eventually, Mrs Le Page was discharged from hospital, and the family was reunited. When John first saw her, he was shocked. His mother's mousy-brown hair had turned white.

During her time away, Mrs Le Page had come to a decision: it was time for them all to move on again. After a year in Halifax, the town held too many sad memories.

John and Betty packed their bags yet again for the journey back down south. In his father's old red briefcase, John carefully stowed his German tail fin.

This time, the family moved to Enfield, a town just north of London, where they stayed with a woman known to the kids as Auntie Vera. She was no blood relation but she did have a 'fraternal' tie to the family. Vera and her husband were members of the Oddfellows, a friendly society that had gathered in Guernsey a few years earlier, when they had first met Mr and Mrs Le Page.

When Vera heard the sad news about John's father, she had written to offer the three of them a place to stay. Her husband was away in the army, she explained, and she and her daughter Beryl could use the company.

The Oddfellows had, in fact, proved invaluable in the months following Mr Le Page's death. As a fully paid-up member, he had been entitled to various benefits, and his surviving family members were to be taken care of financially. Mrs Le Page received ten shillings a week for each of the children for as long as they were still at school.

Socially, too, the Oddfellows looked out for each other. While the Le Pages were staying with Vera, another friend from the society, an older bachelor called Walter, would often come and visit. For John, who was grieving for his father, the male company was welcome.

One day, he and Walter travelled into town together to see the sights, including the Monument commemorating the Great Fire of London. By now, the more recent fires unleashed on the city had all been put out by men like his father, leaving a landscape of historic buildings interspersed with rubble.

The Le Pages didn't stay in Enfield for long. John had barely started at his fourth school in less than two years when his mother announced they were moving again. It was 1944, and the Luftwaffe had returned to London for what was euphemistically called the 'Baby Blitz'.

Operation Steinbock, as it was officially known, saw over 500 bombers raid the capital, as well as targeting cities as far afield as Cardiff, Portsmouth and Hull. In London alone, more than 1,500 people lost their lives – a fraction of the 28,000 killed in the Blitz proper three years earlier but more than enough to alarm Mrs Le Page.

Her sister Frances had long since left Cousin Hilda's house in Devon and was now working for the Admiralty in Bath. The historic city had endured a brief and bloody three-day blitz during the Baedeker raids two years earlier, but the danger had long since passed. 'Come and stay with us,' Frances told her sister. 'There's a lot of bomb damage but it's quiet here now.'

So it was that the family upped sticks yet again, throwing themselves on the mercy of another set of relatives. Compared to busy Halifax and Enfield, the genteel environs of Bath offered a welcome change of pace, although Auntie Frances's small council house, which she shared with her two sons, was a little on the cramped side.

Before long, Mrs Le Page had managed to find herself a job, and with it a new home for her family. She began working as a live-in receptionist for a doctor based on Gay Street, an attractive thoroughfare that led up to The Circus, with its glorious Georgian houses. The doctor and his family spent most of their time at their summer house in nearby Limpley Stoke, so the Le Pages often had the place to themselves.

John immersed himself in yet another new school, taking his eleven-plus exam for a second time. Fortunately, he got the same grade as before. He threw himself into his lessons, in particular the practical ones like carpentry, and made friends with a boy called Richard, who was learning to play the organ at Bath Abbey. John adored sitting in the magnificent fifteenth-century building and listening to the music echoing out of the huge metal pipes.

As time went on, the whole family became more settled in Bath, and for once John's mother made no noises about moving on. She seemed finally to have healed from the wound of her husband's death, and both children were now thriving in their new home.

So it was with slightly mixed feelings that John and his sister greeted the news that the war was finally over, and it was time for the family to return to Guernsey. At thirteen years old, he had spent almost half his life in England and he didn't want to leave.

Five years earlier, the family had caught practically the last boat out of the island. Now, they were on one of the first boats back. But they soon realised that Guernsey wasn't quite ready for a sudden influx of returning evacuees.

John's Uncle Ernie met them at the White Rock, the harbour in downtown St Peter Port from which German prisoners were making their own Channel crossings to the POW camps around England where they would be spending the next couple of years.

After half a decade of occupation, the Germans had certainly left their mark on Guernsey. Convinced that the symbolic value of the Channel Islands would make them a tempting target for the British to retake, Hitler had turned them into the most heavily fortified stretch of his notorious

Atlantic Wall. Looming concrete bunkers dominated the coastline, and minefields, both on land and at sea, now had to be carefully dismantled. John soon grew used to the constant explosions of the mines on the local common being detonated by German prisoners. The large saucer-shaped depressions they left behind remained visible for years, hundreds of tiny blots on the beautiful island landscape.

But for a thirteen-year-old boy, Guernsey had become an explorer's paradise. John loved sneaking around in the abandoned German fortifications, not put off by the fact that most of the bunkers were infested with flies. Most exciting was a huge coastal defence gun that had been mounted at the top of Les Vardes Quarry. The turning mechanism was still in working order, and John enjoyed nothing more than rolling it this way and that, imagining he was firing out to sea. His only regret was that the Germans hadn't left any shells behind.

It wasn't all fun and games, however. At the family home in Vale Parish, there was plenty of work to be done. The years of 'internal trouble' at Lanbury had left the house with lasting damage, so to begin with John and his family stayed with his Aunt Elsa and Uncle Jack, who had remained on the island throughout the war.

Since there was scarcely any food in the shops yet, they relied heavily on their relatives' Red Cross parcels. These regular supplies of essentials, shipped over from Canada and New Zealand, had kept the islanders from starving to death over the past four months, ever since D-Day had cut them off from trade with the Continent. As far as Elsa and Jack were concerned, things were rapidly improving now that the Occupation was over, but John was shocked to hear how much they had struggled while he was away in England.

John had left Guernsey as a boy of eight. Now, at thirteen, he had returned as a man – at least as far as his mother was concerned. Mrs Le Page made it clear that she was relying on John to provide a habitable home for the family. Previously, he had resented the expectation that he should step into his father's shoes, but this was a project that he could happily throw himself into, thanks largely to the practical skills he had picked up at school in Bath.

With a bit of help from their next-door neighbour Cliff, John set about undoing five years' worth of German modifications to the family home, which his dad had built eleven years earlier. The Guernsey authorities stumped up £150 to cover the cost of the repairs, as well as compensating for the value of Mr Le Page's flower boxes and gardening tools, which had mysteriously vanished from the greenhouses. But the job of restoring Lanbury landed squarely on John's thirteen-year-old shoulders. He spent months patching up the broken doors and replacing wooden railings that had been ripped out for firewood. By the time he was finished, Lanbury was as good as new.

After all those years on the mainland, the Le Pages finally had their old house back – but minus the man who had always made it feel like a home.

John had left his father behind in England, buried in Halifax's peaceful Stoney Royd Cemetery. But in his little red briefcase, he still had the old German tail fin, a souvenir of the strange life that he and his family had lived for five years on the far side of the English Channel.

14

IRENE

In many ways, it was the worst-kept secret in history. Only a handful of people knew the details of Operation Overlord, the elaborate Allied plan to open up a 'second front' in Normandy, but pretty much everyone in Britain knew that D-Day was coming. And nowhere was that more true than in Southampton, the historic port city from which more than 100,000 men would soon be leaving for the Continent.

Even four-year-old Irene Brown had realised that something was going on. It was pretty hard not to when there were British soldiers sleeping in your bedroom.

Irene, her mother and her baby brother, Michael, had been turfed out of their usual sleeping quarters and forced to set up camp in their living room instead. Worse still, they were now sharing with her two elder brothers, Peter and Brian, whose bedroom had likewise been requisitioned by the troops.

With thousands of servicemen already based in Southampton preparing for the big day, every room at every inn had been taken. And it wasn't just British soldiers who were cramming themselves into the city. Thousands of

American GIs had also made themselves at home there, the officers billeted in the swanky Polygon Hotel and the rank and file camping on the common.

The 'Yanks' were, as far as little Irene was concerned, an improvement on the home-grown soldiers. They made sure to ingratiate themselves with the local kids, with generous gifts of chocolate and chewing gum. Not for nothing had the phrase 'Got any gum, chum?' entered the local children's vocabulary.

In fact, it was thanks to the Americans that Irene had her first taste of real drinking chocolate. It was a vast improvement on the 'Economy Red Label' she was used to from Cadbury's, which, because of sugar rationing, was now made with artificial sweeteners.

Compared to the Americans, Irene couldn't help feeling that the Tommies who lived with them were rather unfriendly. As they skulked up and down the stairs of the little house on Upper Bugle Street, they never so much as exchanged a word with their host family. Irene didn't even know their names and could barely keep track of how many of them there were.

The men worked around the clock in shifts, based at a command centre in the nearby Saint Michael's Hall. When one soldier got up to go to work, another would take his place on the straw palliasses that covered the floors of the two bedrooms. A constant stream of silent, stony-faced servicemen marched up and down the wooden stairs every day.

At least in the living room Irene and her mother had a double bed to share. The same couldn't be said for the nights they spent in the local air-raid shelter, crammed into a bunk with baby Michael, while her brothers kicked and squirmed in the bunk above them.

Conceived on Mr Brown's last spell of leave from the army, Michael was referred to by Mrs Brown as her husband's 'going-away present'. He was too young to use a child's gas mask like Irene and her elder brothers, so instead, he had his own special baby gas mask, which looked like a diver's helmet and encased all of him except his little legs.

Even three and a half years after the German bombers had first visited the city, Southampton was still the subject of fairly regular air-raid warnings. Irene was used to being woken in the middle of the night by the piercing wail of the siren, scrambling out of bed and rushing down to the shelter, which conveniently enough was right underneath their house.

The shelter was in a large, vaulted cavern known as the Undercroft, which had once been a fourteenth-century shopkeeper's cellar but now provided accommodation for 120 people during air raids. Being so close to the shelter, the Browns usually got the bunks right next to the door, which meant they could nip out again quickly as soon as the all clear sounded.

Little Irene was well practised in the night-time routine. She had only the dimmest idea of why they went down there, aware that it was something to do with the reason

Daddy had left his job in the docks to join the army. There was always music playing in the shelter, conspicuously loudly to drown out the sound of the planes.

The Browns had been sheltering in the Undercroft for more than three years now – not that Irene's recollections stretched back that far. Mercifully, she had no memory of the blitz visited on the city in the winter of 1940, in which hundreds of people had been killed and tens of thousands of properties damaged. Irene had been just a babe in arms, around Michael's age, when the scullery at the back of the family's old house in Brunswick Square was hit by a German mine.

Miraculously, the mine had failed to go off. While the police and ARP wardens cordoned off the area, Mrs Brown had rushed her children away to safety. They had stayed at a house in Swanage, a sleepy seaside town fifty miles away on the Dorset coast. But a few weeks in the countryside had been more than Irene's mother could cope with. She longed for her own home again, and for her hometown.

Mrs Brown had never lived away from Southampton, the city her own parents had come to when they left Ireland three decades earlier. During their first few months in England, all five of the kids they brought with them had died of diphtheria – five siblings that she had never met – but in Southampton her parents had started a new brood. Irene's mother was one of fourteen in the large Catholic family. To her, Southampton just felt right. Despite the bombs, she wanted to go back.

But when the family returned, the house in Brunswick Square was still uninhabitable. After a brief spell of homelessness, when they slept in the Undercroft every night, they moved into their new home, directly above it.

The two-bedroom house was a stone's throw from the docks, on the corner of Simnel Street opposite the Titanic pub, named for the ship that had begun its ill-fated voyage less than a mile away. Irene loved it there, Tommies or no Tommies, and she always felt safe playing hopscotch outside in the road, watched over by the neighbourhood's 'aunties' and 'grannies'.

It was a close-knit community, and everyone looked out for each other. One time, when a homeless man was found sleeping on the street, one of the neighbours gave him some old clothes to change into, while someone else brewed him up a cup of tea and a third brought out a bowl of hot water for him to wash with.

In fact, Mrs Brown's generosity was legendary in the neighbourhood. Whenever she cooked up a stew or got hold of a pig's head to boil up into brawn, Irene would be sent round to all the elderly 'grannies' in the street to collect a bowl from each of them, which she would bring back with a hearty helping of Mrs Brown's latest dish.

When it came to her own family, though, Irene's mother was more sparing. Like most children, Irene had a sweet tooth and she would gaze longingly at the jar of sweeties her mother kept out of reach in the kitchen. She and her brothers were limited to no more than one sweet a day, and woe betide any child who tried to take more than their share.

In her husband's absence, Mrs Brown had become stricter than ever, not averse to slapping her children if she caught them misbehaving or clouting them round the ear if they ever dared give her cheek. She also expected them to help around the house. Every week, she would put Irene to work scrubbing the hallway and beating the rug with a broom, while Brian and Peter washed the windows and cleaned the front steps. Her door was always open to any neighbour who fancied a cup of tea and a natter, and it was important that the house looked spick and span.

But Mrs Brown's strictest rule was that everyone should come when they were summoned, an essential condition in wartime when the siren could go off at any minute. The moment Irene heard her mum's shrill voice calling her name, she would hop right back home again on the double. When Mrs Brown told you to come in, she meant *now*.

Irene and her brothers were under strict instructions not to stray too far from the house. But they were lucky that the land around Upper Bugle Street provided an inviting playground, thanks to a large bomb-damaged wasteland around the back of St Michael's Church, which was gradually becoming overgrown.

It was on this sprawling, wild landscape that Irene and the other girls in the neighbourhood would play 'house', sweeping away the weeds and debris and making their patch of the ruins as tidy as possible, while the boys played war games in the rubble.

It had never occurred to Irene to ask why exactly the houses that had once stood on the wasteland had fallen down. She had only the vaguest understanding of the war and what it had done to her city. At home, her mother always brushed aside questions on the subject. Whenever one of her brothers tried to ask something at the dinner table, she would shut them up with a brisk 'Eat your food!'

One day, after lunch, Irene and her brothers went over to the bombsite together. There were no other girls around that afternoon but the boys agreed she could play with them. Irene knew she wouldn't be the first choice of playmate for lads of seven and eight, so she was pleased to be included in the game.

'It's Cowboys and Indians,' Brian told her. 'We're the cowboys and you're the Indian.'

He picked up a piece of rope that was lying on the ground and led Irene over to a nearby tree. 'We've captured you,' he told her as he fastened her tightly to the trunk, wrapping the rope around her waist and tying it expertly with a knot. 'Don't worry, we'll be back in a minute.'

Then the boys ran off.

A minute passed and they didn't come back. Five minutes . . . Ten minutes . . . An hour.

Irene was getting scared. She began to call out, but there was no one around. The wasteland was bordered by what was left of an old wall and no one outside it could see in without peering over the top.

Hours passed, and Irene watched the sun sink in the sky. By now she was in tears and screaming for help at the top of her lungs.

When she needed to go to the toilet, she held it in as long as she could, but eventually there was nothing she could do but wet herself.

Then, at last, she heard voices on the other side of the wall. One of them belonged to an old man. The other one sounded familiar. It was her mother!

'There's a little girl down there crying,' Irene heard the old man say.

Moments later Mrs Brown was striding across the wasteland, with a look of thunder on her face.

'How long have you been here for?' she asked Irene as she loosened the rope around her waist.

'Since we came out to play,' her daughter replied.

'But that was one o'clock!' Mrs Brown exclaimed. She looked at her watch. 'It's nearly five now.'

The two of them walked back to Upper Bugle Street together, where they waited for the boys to return home. When they did, Irene watched with glee as Mrs Brown bent each of them over her knee and thwacked them for all she was worth. Then she sent them both to bed with no supper.

Irene laughed. 'You won't do that again,' she said as the boys skulked off, rubbing their backsides.

*

With her husband away, Mrs Brown had to be mother and father to her children. But even when he was back home from the army, Irene's father wasn't much of a disciplinarian. In fact, he was something of a child himself. Fun-loving and full of energy, he was popular with all the kids on Upper Bugle Street and would often play out in the road with them when the other parents had all gone inside. 'Is Mr Brown coming out tonight?' the local kids would ask Irene hopefully, whenever they knew that her father was home on leave.

Mr Brown loved all three of his children, but Irene was the apple of his eye and he always called her 'Daddy's girl'. She looked forward to his visits, when her mum would blow a week's worth of ration coupons on a slap-up homecoming meal.

Mrs Brown insisted the kids never stray far from the family home, but their dad would happily walk with them into town. One day he took them along the high street to the common, where the American troops had pitched their tents. On the way, they passed dozens of gaping holes where shops and houses should have been, and this time Irene couldn't help asking what had happened to them.

'Oh, don't worry about them,' her dad told her. 'Those buildings were very old.'

Unfortunately, with D-Day approaching, Mr Brown announced he would soon be leaving again. Irene was sad to see him go and she worried about what he would be doing in France. She knew now that soldiers like Daddy would be fighting the Germans, bad people whom her brothers nicknamed 'square heads'. Irene imagined an army of monstrous creatures with large blocks set upon their shoulders.

There was one consolation, however. Around the same time that Mr Brown left to prepare for the invasion, the British soldiers who had been billeted with the family packed up as well, and Irene and her mother were able to reclaim their bedroom upstairs, even if baby Michael hadn't yet mastered sleeping through the night.

The Americans in Southampton, too, were clearly gearing up for the big day. Irene watched them packing up their tents and loading their lorries, wearing slightly more serious expressions than usual on their handsome, well-fed faces.

Soon, American vehicles seemed to be everywhere as they lined up in convoy along the Western Esplanade. The invasion wasn't just sending men over to France but machinery as well. More than 200,000 tanks, Jeeps and staff cars would soon be making their way to the Continent.

One afternoon, Irene was startled by a deafening grinding noise from the street outside. She leapt out of her chair to find the floor seemed to be shaking beneath her feet. She ran to find her mother and together they went to investigate.

Outside, a thirty-ton Sherman tank was embedded in the brick wall of the Undercroft. The driver must have misjudged the distance coming round the corner from Simnel Street, mounting the pavement and then clipping the wall as he turned. If the tank carried on going any further, it was liable to take out their front steps.

Irene and her mother watched in astonishment as a young GI leapt out of a jeep parked up a little further along the road and ran back to alert the tank driver, who had evidently been following him around the corner. He clambered up on the roof of the tank and began hammering with his fist on the hatch. It popped open, and the head of another, rather startled GI emerged.

The two men conferred for a few moments before the hatch went down again and the hulking vehicle began jiggling back and forth, attempting to dislodge itself from the crumbling masonry. Irene felt the house shudder again.

With a bit of help from his colleague, the tank driver was able to extricate his vehicle without causing any serious damage. Soon, he was on his way, his blushes hidden behind two-inch-thick walls of steel.

With only a slit to see out of, it was no surprise that he had struggled to navigate Southampton's narrow medieval streets. And perhaps it was just as well that he couldn't hear much of what was going on outside either, since it meant he was spared Mrs Brown's expletive-filled commentary on his driving skills.

As the American vehicles lined up along the Esplanade, Irene and the other children ran out to bid them farewell. She assumed they must be going back home to America and felt it was only polite to say goodbye.

The Americans, for their part, were more generous than ever, showering the kids with not just candy and chocolate bars but whatever English money they had left in their pockets. For Irene and her friends it was quite a windfall.

On 6 June 1944, the *Southampton Echo* published the news that nearly everyone in the town had already deduced for themselves. 'Allies Land in Northern France' the paper proclaimed. 'Free Men Marching Together to Victory.'

The latter was a quotation from General Eisenhower's 'Order of the Day', a personal message to the 175,000 troops taking part in Operation Overlord, which the newspaper had reproduced in full.

'The tide has turned,' the supreme commander declared. 'We will accept nothing less than full victory.'

But as the boats began returning to Southampton later in the day, the local people saw another side of Operation Overlord: the large number of casualties brought back to England with injuries sustained on the 'far shore'. Once again, Irene ran down to the waterfront to see what was happening, although this time the mood was more sombre. Over the ensuing months more than 100,000 casualties would return to England via Southampton, to be treated in hospitals all along the south coast.

Before long, it wasn't just Allied soldiers arriving in the bustling port city. One day a large group of German prisoners was unloaded at the Royal Pier and marched towards a POW camp on the common.

Irene and her brothers went to gawp at them, curious to see the enemy up close. She was surprised to discover that they didn't have square heads at all. In fact, they looked like fairly ordinary young men, just rather exhausted and bedraggled. Irene wasn't sure what all the fuss was about.

Irene still had little idea about what her father was doing on the Continent, although as the months went by a string of exotic presents arrived by post, offering clues to where he was stationed. A postcard with a little French flag on it, toys for her brothers that bore the labels *'fabriqué en Belgique'* or *'gemaakt in Nederland'*. Finally, a little pink tea set all the way from Germany.

Mrs Brown would always listen intently to the latest news on the wireless, ushering the kids out of the room when the BBC broadcasts began. More than once, Irene watched her brothers get a clout round the ear when they tried to listen in at the keyhole. She knew better than to try anything similar herself.

But during Mr Brown's longest absence yet, the family did have another man in the house – a young American GI called Bobby, who arrived with his new British bride, Anne. They had met and married in London, joining the ranks of 70,000 transatlantic newlyweds who had made it down the aisle – despite plenty of obstacles thrown in their way by parents, priests and even the US Army.

Now, Bobby had been transferred to Southampton, and he and his new wife needed somewhere to stay.

'I'll need to see your marriage certificate,' Mrs Brown told him. She had heard plenty of stories of 'hanky-panky' between the Yanks and foolish local girls, and the last thing she wanted was trouble under her roof.

Fortunately, Bobby was prepared for such questioning. 'Sure thing,' he replied cheerfully, handing over the necessary documentation for Mrs Brown to scrutinise.

'All right then,' she said. 'You two can have the front room.'

Bobby and Anne were a picture-perfect couple. He was tall and dark-haired, the model of a well-built American serviceman. She was a stylish blonde, who took the wartime slogan 'beauty is your duty' very seriously. But they were also the ideal houseguests, polite, respectful, helpful and friendly. It was a far cry from the Browns' previous experience with the tight-lipped English Tommies. In the evening, Bobby would sit playing cards with the kids at the dining-room table, and in the daytime, while he was out at work, Mrs Brown and Anne would sit out on the front step, nattering over endless cups of tea.

Try as he might, Bobby had failed to get Irene's mother hooked on the top-quality ground coffee that he brought home from the American Army's Post Exchange. But Irene and her brothers were easier to please. With her sweet tooth, Irene had always had a soft spot for the Americans, but the 'candy' and chewing gum she had scored off them in the past were nothing compared to the cornucopia of delights Bobby brought home with him. Huge Hershey's chocolate bars, fistfuls of sweeties and, on one occasion, a traditional American treat that surpassed Irene's wildest dreams.

She and her brothers were sitting around the dining table playing Snap when they heard the young soldier's cheerful rap on the door. 'Good evening, Mrs Brown,' he greeted her mother politely. 'I hope you don't mind but I've brought something for the children.'

Bobby plonked a huge cardboard box down on the table. 'Here you are, gang!' he told the kids. 'Help yourselves.'

Irene didn't need to be told twice. She leapt at the package, tearing it open to reveal its precious contents: a tray full of fat, glistening doughnuts. She grabbed one in her hand and bit into it, thrilled to discover that it was filled with delicious strawberry jam.

'Oh, I do wish you wouldn't, Bobby,' Irene's mother chastised him. But there was a smile in her eyes when she said it.

Before long, there was no more 'Mrs Brown' either. Irene's mother insisted that Bobby and Anne both call her 'Mum'.

To Irene, it seemed like the most natural thing in the world. After just a few months, Bobby and Anne really did feel like family.

The long-awaited D-Day might have finally come and gone, but even as the new Western Front moved eastwards there was no shortage of Americans in Southampton. The US Army's 14th Major Port Transportation Corps had taken over the harbour and was responsible for supplying the front lines with food, medicines and materiel. By the end of the year, 19 million pounds of fruit and veg had passed through the port on its way to the French shore, along with 220,000 vehicles and more than a million men.

While their colleagues on the Continent fought their way inch by inch towards Germany, the Americans who remained behind in England were living the good life. In October 1944, 5,000 GIs – along with some very confused locals – attended the first American football game played on British soil. A few months later, the gym at a local school was given over to a basketball tournament.

Bobby enjoyed sport but his and Anne's real passion was dancing. In the evenings they would go out jiving at the local Red Cross Club, and when the new American music played on the radio, they would demonstrate their moves to the kids at home too. They never offered to teach Irene and her brothers how to dance, though, wary of offending Mrs Brown's strict sense of propriety.

The winter of 1944 was a bitterly cold one, and for the Browns – like many families up and down the country – it had a sad undercurrent as well. Irene's father was some-where out in Europe, and in his usual place at the head of the table, her mum had placed a photograph of him instead.

She had, at least, managed to rustle up a decent Christmas dinner, thanks to a deal she had made with the local butcher. The past few weeks, Mrs Brown had spent much of her time at the kitchen table, covered in feathers from the seemingly endless stream of chickens she had been plucking. Her reward for all this hard work was that she got to keep one of the birds for her own family.

There might not be much in the way of presents, but the Browns had all made a big effort to make that Christmas as festive as could be. They had got hold of a real tree, and decorated it with shining milk bottle tops, threaded on string to make little bells. Mrs Brown had wrapped up little parcels of sweeties in brown paper and hung them on the tree as well, for the kids to munch on when the meal was over.

Irene missed her father, but she took solace in the thought that she would see him again soon. Even a child of five knew the war couldn't last forever.

Sure enough, five months later came the news that everyone had been waiting for. Hitler was dead and Allied troops were entering Berlin.

When Bobby announced that it was time to go back to America, Irene was sorry to see him go. But he promised to come and see them in a few months' time, when he returned to fetch Anne back home with him. In the meantime, she would go and stay with her parents up in London.

There was only one homecoming on Irene's mind, though: her father's. When the big day finally arrived, she threw herself into his arms.

But not everyone in the family was as excited to see Mr Brown. Little Michael, now approaching two years old, had no memory of the stranger who had suddenly appeared in the doorway. He screamed and went to hide behind his mother's legs.

In time, the Browns adjusted to postwar life, just happy that they had all made it through the war in one piece. Irene knew that not all children had been so fortunate. Many had lost their fathers during the war years, or got them back irreparably damaged in body or spirit.

Mr Brown returned to his old work as a stevedore on the docks and seemed to pick up pretty much where he had left off all those years earlier. He would make the occasional passing reference to good mates he had lost in the army, but whatever horrors he had experienced on the Continent had done nothing to dim his good humour.

Once the Americans had returned to their hometowns, attention had gradually turned to the plight of the tens of thousands of British women waiting to join them. In December 1945, the US Congress passed the War Brides Act, offering non-quota immigration status to the spouses of former American servicemen.

But when Bobby returned to bring Anne home with him, he encountered a problem. She was sick, with a lung problem that sounded suspiciously like TB. He wasn't sure the US authorities would let her in.

Bobby began making arrangements to smuggle his wife in via Canada, but Anne was resolute: she didn't want to break the rules. As long as she was contagious, she was determined that she would stay in London.

It was a long time before Bobby returned to Southampton as he had promised, and when he did, it was far from a happy reunion. He had come to share some sad news with Mrs Brown.

Irene's mother filled the children in later that evening. 'It's Anne,' she told them tearfully. 'She's gone up to live with the angels.'

Irene felt a wave of sadness overcome her, and she could tell that her mother was feeling it too. 'She was such a beautiful girl,' Mrs Brown said wistfully. 'No one loved life the way she did.'

With the blessing of his English 'mum', Bobby was returning to America, where he was determined to make a fresh start. Mrs Brown sent him on his way with all her hopes for a happier future.

For Irene and her brothers, Anne's death was a stark reminder that they were the lucky ones. Wartime or not, tragedy could strike at any time.

15

PAT

Phut . . . phut . . . phut . . .

Throughout the summer of 1944, that sound was enough to send a chill down any Londoner's spine. For the men, women and children living in the capital who endured attack from over 10,000 V-1 'flying bombs' launched from sites in northern France, the intermittent noise of the jet engine firing was a regular menace.

It had earned these primitive cruise missiles, which looked like little pilotless aircraft, with a wingspan of just seventeen feet, a set of nicknames that were already known to every schoolchild. Compared to the official German name *Vergeltungswaffe 1* ('vengeance weapon 1'), the British colloquialisms had an innocent charm: initially known as 'buzz bombs', they later acquired the even cuter nickname 'doodlebugs'.

The grown-ups, meanwhile, had their own more risqué terminology for the pilotless aircraft: 'farting fannies', on account of the noise they made. Or, in some more ribald quarters, 'Hitler's virgins' ('because no man had ever been inside them').

The only thing worse than the noise the doodlebugs made as they were flying overhead was the silence when the engine cut out. Then you knew it was only a matter of seconds before the missile fell from the sky and detonated its 850kg warhead, leaving a crater up to twenty metres wide and generating a blast that could blow out windows several streets away. A single V-1 could damage up to 400 houses, and the noise of the explosion could be heard for miles.

At seven years old, Londoner Pat Peacham was used to the sight and, more crucially, the sound of the so-called 'vengeance weapons'. Living in West Ham, she had seen her fair share of them already. Several times her father had brought her up on the roof of the Anderson shelter he had built in their back yard to watch as the RAF made their last-ditch efforts to crash the bombs before they arrived in densely populated areas.

By late July 1944, a wave of defences had been set up to protect the people of London. There were pilots to engage the V-1s as they crossed the Channel from their launch sites in France and Holland, an array of anti-aircraft guns on the south coast to shoot them down as they passed through their sights, and finally a thity-five-mile-long strip of barrage balloons around the capital's south-eastern flank, which became known as 'the Goalkeepers of London'.

But despite the combined efforts of the RAF pilots, Anti-Aircraft Command and the operators of the barrage balloon sites – who often found themselves ducking for cover as a V-1 got caught up in their cables and crashed to the ground – more than 6,000 doodlebugs still made it through to the capital, leaving hundreds of thousands of Londoners homeless. The problem was that with such a big target – London was more than twenty miles across – even their rudimentary guidance systems were enough to ensure they always hit something, or someone.

Occasionally, the V-1s approached the capital with British fighters still on their tails. One day, Pat and her father watched, thrilled, as an RAF Mosquito – the only plane fast enough to match the doodlebug's 400 mph top speed – caught up with one, brought its wing tip to bear on the flying bomb and successfully 'tipped' it off course, causing it to detonate in a relatively unpopulated area. It was daring aerial manoeuvres such as this that led to the air force's defence against the V-1 menace being nicknamed 'the Second Battle of Britain'.

Pat had heard plenty of sinister tales of local people being killed by the flying bombs. Not only those blasted to pieces or buried under rubble but the stranger cases of men and women snuffed out by the terrible shockwaves that accompanied each blast. One local family, so the story went, had been sitting around their dining-room table when a doodlebug detonated nearby. Their dead bodies were discovered sitting bolt upright in their chairs, as if they had been turned to stone.

Not that Pat was unduly worried. At seven years old, she had little concept of danger. Her mother and her aunts might be a bundle of nerves whenever they heard the air-raid siren go off, but she was used to simply taking it in her stride. For as long as she could remember, Pat had been grabbed, bundled and shoved into one supposedly safe place or another whenever the familiar whine began – under beds, tables, whatever was closest to hand. One time, she was unceremoniously placed inside a cupboard, where she curled up patiently, waiting for the all clear to sound.

The family's Anderson shelter, which Mr Peacham had carefully built in the yard out back, was the obvious place to be during an air raid – but of all the options available, it was in many ways the least appealing. Pat's father had covered the corrugated-iron roof in grass, thinking that would make it look inconspicuous from the air, but as a result it was prone to flooding and attracted a disproportionate number of insects. His wife wasn't sure which she was more scared of falling on her head: a German bomb or a native English earwig.

Mrs Peacham was houseproud by nature and her own home was always spotless. When her sisters and their kids were evacuated to Cheshire in 1940, she and Pat had gone to visit them there. But the louse-infested beds they were expected to sleep in were too much for Mrs Peacham. She packed up and went straight back home again.

When it came to the air raids, though, she put up with the dank environs of the Anderson shelter, sitting with Pat on a little raised bunk bed so as to keep their feet out of the water that pooled on the floor. Her sister Ethel lived in the house next door, and Ethel's husband, Frank, was the local

ARP warden, spending his evenings going round the local neighbourhood telling everyone to get inside their shelters.

Frank wasn't a man you wanted to cross. A difficult childhood had left him angry and bitter, and even little Pat was familiar with the results. His poor mongrel dog always seemed to bear the brunt of his rage, being thwacked and kicked whenever Uncle Frank was in one of his moods.

Pat had a soft spot for animals. One day, after watching the local rag-and-bone man beating his decrepit old pony, she had rushed home and burst into tears. At least her uncle's dog lived close enough that she could offer it some comfort. When she was sure Frank wasn't looking, she would creep over the fence and shower the little animal with kisses and cuddles.

Pat adored her Aunt Ethel, but she hated Uncle Frank. Something about the way her aunt always rushed back home anxiously when she knew that her husband was expecting her made Pat wonder if the dog wasn't the only one on the receiving end of her uncle's temper.

Fortunately, Pat had no shortage of relatives in the neighbourhood, and most of them were a lot nicer than Uncle Frank. Her mother was one of ten children, and nearly all of them lived within walking distance of each other. In addition to Frank and Ethel, Pat's grandparents as well as her Aunt Violet and her family also lived on their street.

Pat herself was an only child – though not, it seemed, for lack of trying on her parents' part. No one had ever mentioned the possibility of her having a sibling, but she had noted the large pram and pair of cots that arrived in the passageway one day, and then disappeared without comment a few weeks later. This routine had been repeated a couple of times before the baby gear was finally removed for good.

Pat's parents never spoke to her about it. They weren't the kind of family that went in for emotional conversations. In fact, the most heated Pat ever saw her mother get was when her father was in the midst of one of his regular gambling spells. Mr Peacham was a low-key addict, more than capable of blowing both his own wages, earned as a lagger on the docks, and what his wife brought in from her job at a local furrier's. Every week, he would count out his wages in the toilet before handing over as much as he thought Mrs Peacham would need for housekeeping. The rest would go on the dog tracks in West Ham and Romford.

At times, Pat was her father's accomplice when he needed to place a discreet wager. He would slip her some money and a piece of paper with the name of his favoured dog scrawled on it and ask her to take it to the bookie's runner down the road. He never told Pat whether or not the bet came up trumps, but he must have been lucky at least some of the time since the family was unusually well-equipped with all the latest mod cons. They were the first in the street to have a radiogram, and later, the first to get a television too – a black-and-white Sobel in a beautiful wooden cabinet – even if the screen was only a few inches wide.

The houseproud Mrs Peacham couldn't resist keeping up with the Joneses – or, more accurately, being the one everyone else in the neighbourhood struggled to keep up with. She went through so many pieces of furniture, always gifting the old unwanted sofas and chairs to one of her siblings, that when Pat went round to visit her relatives' houses she often had a feeling of *déjà vu*. Wherever she went, it seemed, there was something she recognised from home.

But like all gamblers, Mr Peacham's luck rarely held out for long. Pat's family never quite sank to the depths of the local rag-and-bone man, whose kids would go around in just their vests and pants because he'd been forced to pawn their clothes, but when Mr Peacham was reduced to raiding his sister-in-law's gas meter for pennies and cooking kippers over a candle, his wife felt enough was enough. One night, Pat's mother dragged her out all around the docks in search of her father and his gambling pals, determined to catch him in the act and shame him into giving it up. Unfortunately, they didn't manage to find him. Pat waited anxiously for her dad to come back home, anticipating the angry exchanges that would follow.

Gambling aside, Mr Peacham was a devoted husband – and as far as Pat was concerned, a pretty decent father as well. On Sundays, he would treat her with a visit to the docks, where she watched with fascination as the pistons in the great ships' engine rooms went back and forth. On the way home, Pat would generally be parked outside a pub with a glass of lemonade and a packet of crisps while her dad fitted in a quick game of cards.

Mr Peacham made no secret of the fact that he had always wanted to have a son, but he was more than happy to share his manly skills with his daughter instead. He taught Pat to make herself a go-kart out of wood, scrounging spare wheels from the neighbours' old prams and even using a red-hot poker to make the holes through which to attach the nuts and bolts.

Concerns about health and safety were relatively low on the family agenda. As long as the German bombs weren't falling from the sky, Pat was trusted to take care of herself. She spent her days with the other kids from her street, playing in the bombsites, swinging on the gas pipes hanging from the ceiling of the all-but-obliterated local church and baking potatoes over campfires in the rubble. By the time she came home in the evening, there was just time for a quick meal and then it was off to bed. The arrangement suited Mrs Peacham well, since having children running around inside the house was a sure way for things to get messy.

One night, when Pat stayed over at the home of one of the other girls in the street, she was surprised to find that things were done very differently there. The girl's father tucked them both in at night, before kissing them gently on the forehead. To Pat, that kind of affection was completely alien. She loved her parents, and she knew that they loved her, but they might as well have lived in different worlds.

When she wasn't keeping house, Mrs Peacham, along with most of her siblings, was a committed party-goer –

and in her upbeat, gregarious husband, who had developed a fine line in card tricks, she had found a man who slotted into her extended family perfectly. Every weekend there was either a trip to the pub, or a 'do' at the home of one of Pat's aunts or uncles. The most convenient local boozer was the King's Head on Church Street, which had a large green outside where the family could play rounders while they waited for the doors to open in the early evening.

When they did, Mrs Peacham and her siblings would gather round the old pub piano. Everyone in the family had their favourite tune: 'Rolling Round the World', 'Carolina in the Morning', 'Bring Me a Letter from My Old Home Town'.

Pat's own favourite song was 'I'm Looking Over a Four Leaf Clover'. She had been practising on the piano at home – an exquisite Steinway upright, light walnut with green edging and beautiful mother-of-pearl keys. But while her more confident relatives seemed to be born performers, Pat never dared play in public.

Once the pub closed, air raids permitting, everyone would go back to one of the siblings' houses for a proper East End knees-up. When it all got too much for Pat, she'd retreat to the cellar, watching the floorboards above her head jiggle up and down as the grown-ups danced.

The whole family, it seemed, were committed to squeezing as much fun out of life as they could. Even her grandfather Joe would get in on the action. No party was complete without a performance of his legendary 'Egyptian dance'. After a bit of salt was thrown on the floor to represent the desert, he would wrap a towel around his head, strip down to his long johns and shuffle up and down the room, one hand jutting out in front of him and the other behind.

The biggest bashes of all, though, took place at Auntie Kitty's house in Waltham Cross. Her next-door neighbour was equally fun-loving and the two houses were always thrown open all night long, with revellers free to pass back and forth between them. Pat's parents and their friends in West Ham would hire the local coal merchant's lorry for the evening, sweeping the coal dust out of the back of it and then bringing their wooden kitchen chairs to sit on as they rattled along on the twelve-mile journey. Dusting their fine fur coats off at the other end, they always made a spectacular entrance.

For Pat, though, the constant partying was all a bit much. She preferred a trip to the pictures to staying up late into the night with her huge extended family. But at least she wasn't entirely alone in that. Although most of her cousins were a good decade older than her, and already on the cusp of adulthood themselves, her mum's sister Nell did have a boy her own age: Terry.

As the babies of the family, Pat and Terry naturally gravitated towards each other, and Pat was never happier than when they could sneak off to play together rather than joining in with the rest of the throng.

During the war, Terry's stepfather, Jack, was away serving with the Special Boat Service. The two of them had never quite seen eye to eye, although Terry owed Jack a great debt. Jack had married Terry's mother, Nell, knowing she was already pregnant with another man's child. If it hadn't been for this act of generosity, Terry would have been given up for adoption.

Jack wasn't exactly a jolly character but he did his best to join in with his wife's ebullient family. One Christmas, he had volunteered to play the role of Santa, covered in red crepe paper from head to foot and sporting a long white beard made of cotton wool.

When Jack entered the living room in his costume, everyone cheered, but as he bent down to hand one of the children a present he got too close to the lit candles that decorated the tree. The crepe paper caught alight, and within seconds his backside was on fire. It took a massive effort on the part of his in-laws to stop themselves laughing long enough to extinguish the flames.

There were certainly advantages to coming from such a big family. As much as Pat felt her own parents were less affectionate than those of some of her friends, she had more surrogate mums and dads than she knew what to do with. Mrs Peacham's siblings had all looked after each other's children for decades, and as the babies of the family, Pat and Terry were no exception. Pat was frequently sent to stay with her Aunt Ivy and Uncle Fred in Richmond, while Terry was a regular fixture at Aunt Kitty's house in Waltham Cross.

One time, Aunt Kitty agreed to have the two of them for an extended six-week visit. To begin with they were left at home during the daytime, while their aunt and uncle were out at work, but after Pat and Terry spent a whole day playing records on the wind-up gramophone in the living room, they incurred the wrath of one of the neighbours. The old lady next door was used to the noise of Kitty's frequent all-night parties, but music in the daytime was a step too far.

From then on, Pat and Terry were locked out of the house from dawn to dusk and forced to make their own entertainment. Many of their days were spent fishing in the local canal before dragging their catch of tiddlers home with them in an old tin bath. Most of the fish had already begun to rot by the time they made it back for tea, so the day's catch didn't help much with their aunt's meal planning.

Unlike Pat, Terry had already been bombed out once during the war, although he was too young to remember it. Four years earlier, back in the autumn of 1940, he and his parents had been cooped up in their Anderson shelter in the back yard when the Luftwaffe deposited a landmine on their front doorstep. Their house, and several around it, were rendered uninhabitable and they were forced to move to a new home on the next street along.

There the family had suffered a loss of a much smaller kind, but no less distressing to young Terry. After one particularly nasty raid, he emerged from the Anderson shelter to find their pet cat lying dead in the drain, having been fatally wounded by a piece of shrapnel.

Both Pat and Terry had seen plenty of dead animals since the bombing had started – especially cats, which were hard to keep track of and seemed to use up their nine lives very quickly. But until the Doodlebug Summer of 1944, they had seen few of the war's human victims.

One afternoon, Pat and her mother were visiting Auntie Violet down the road, and Terry had been sent by his mother to join them. It was about half a mile from his house to Auntie Violet's, but he hadn't got more than halfway before he was stopped in his tracks by a sinister noise overhead.

Terry looked up to see a dark object flying towards him, with the unmistakable silhouette of a doodlebug.

He froze, transfixed by the sight. The sirens hadn't even started wailing when he heard the *phut-phut-phutting* suddenly give out, and the flying bomb began its steep descent.

Travelling at up to 400 miles an hour, the doodlebugs could take between five and fifteen seconds to hit the ground, but for little Terry those few moments felt like an age. He was vaguely aware of someone running towards him and looked over to see a woman waving her arms and shouting, 'My children! My children!'

Wherever her children were, she wasn't going to get to them in time, but when the woman reached Terry, she grabbed hold of him and pulled him into a tight embrace. He looked up into eyes that were white with terror.

Then the flying bomb hit the ground and exploded, showering them both with mortar and debris.

Terry, still looking up at the stranger, saw something sharp and grey embed itself in her forehead. When a red trickle of blood began to flow from the wound, he clamped his eyes shut tight.

Deafened by the blast, Terry couldn't hear the engine of the builders' lorry that sped round the corner moments later, nor the shouts of the two men who helped the injured woman into the back before driving her off to hospital. Before he knew it, he was left standing alone in the street again, as the dust and ash whirled around him.

Terry started running and he didn't stop until he reached his Aunt Violet's house. When he arrived, he found Pat and her mother standing on the doorstep, aghast at the explosion they had just witnessed. Auntie Violet's house was intact but many others in the street were not. People were running up and down the road, shouting and screaming. Pat saw a bus conductress rushing past in her smart navy-blue uniform, holding a bloodied handkerchief up to her face. She only needed the briefest glimpse to see that the woman's eye had been blown right out of its socket.

Poor Terry, who had raced the last part of the journey as quickly as his little legs would carry him, collapsed on the doorstep, shaking like a leaf. When he looked back at the cloud of smoke rising in the distance, he began to wail, convinced that his own house, where his mother and baby brother were, had been hit. It was all Mrs Peacham could do to calm him down, explaining that the curve of the road only made it look that way, and in fact the bomb had fallen a safe distance away from their home.

For her part, Pat's mother was more worried about her own house. Once Terry had caught his breath and calmed down a little, she set off to inspect the damage, with both kids in tow. Pat gawped at the sight of their bay window, shattered by the shockwave, but it was clear the harm to the house was relatively superficial. In fact, it was still habitable, broadly speaking – although not exactly up to Mrs Peacham's usual standards – and that was more than could be said for many of their neighbours' properties. Further up the road, several houses had been completely obliterated.

By now, a crowd of people was making its way up the road, heading towards the spot the smoke was rising from. Pat and Terry followed Mrs Peacham as she joined the throng converging on the point of impact. Whatever buildings had once stood there had been reduced to a pile of rubble, and volunteers were already hard at work sifting through it in search of survivors.

But for those at ground zero, the chances of survival were negligible. Pat watched, grimly fascinated, as a man in a smart sailor's uniform emerged, carrying an old lady in his arms. From the way her tongue was lolling out of her mouth, it was obvious even to Pat that she was dead.

When he had laid her gently down on the ground, the sailor returned to the bombsite, digging at the rubble with his hands. This time he found a much smaller body. It was a little boy, around the same age as Pat and Terry. Pat couldn't make out what he was wearing thanks to the layer of grey dust covering his body, but she thought she caught a glimpse of something blue. She was pretty sure she didn't know him, although he couldn't have lived far away from her.

As the boy's limp body was laid down on the ground, Pat's eyes were drawn to his hair. It was thick with dust from the explosion, matted and grey like a dirty mop.

'Come on,' Mrs Peacham said quietly, leading Pat and Terry back down the road to Auntie Violet's house.

Terry returned home later that afternoon, relieved to find his mother and baby brother still in one piece. Pat and her mum, meanwhile, went to deal with the damage to their own home. A tarpaulin was draped over what was left of the front window to keep out the rain, while they waited for a team of builders provided by the council to arrive and begin the repair work.

When they did eventually appear, the men seemed to take forever to finish the job. One afternoon Mrs Peacham arrived home from work early and found out why. Two of the builders were downstairs in the front room, listening to the radio with their feet up. The others were on the landing above, playing hoopla with a couple of horseshoes, having banged several six-inch nails into the floorboards to use as targets.

Pat couldn't make out much of the furious language that Mrs Peacham hurled at the workmen. All she knew was that a few minutes later they were all out in the street, and they never returned. From now on, Pat's dad would be in charge of the repair project. He had already proved his talent for DIY by building a lean-to out the back to house the family toilet, complete with net curtains – surely, the next best thing to actually bringing 'the facilities' indoors. Patching up a bit of bomb damage was well within his abilities.

The doodlebug raid had been a close shave for Pat and her family, but in the months that followed the neighbourhood continued to suffer from Hitler's flying bombs. It wasn't until early 1945 that the threat from V-1s receded, as the Allied soldiers on the Continent overran the last of their launch sites. Although some doodlebugs continued to be released mid-air by German Heinkels, the threat to London had all but disappeared.

By then, 6,000 Londoners had been killed by the flying bombs, and another 18,000 seriously injured. The loss of habitable housing ran into the hundreds of thousands.

But Hitler wasn't done with his 'vengeance weapons'. As the V-1 threat receded, another even more terrifying menace took its place. The V-2 was a 14m rocket that travelled faster than the speed of sound, making the 200-mile journey from launch site to target in just over five minutes. There was no way of intercepting or stopping it, and no real warning that it was coming. When it made impact, and its 900kg payload detonated, the explosion was powerful enough to damage up to 750 houses in one fell swoop.

At first, the seemingly random explosions that began occurring all over London in the autumn of 1944 were put down to gas-main explosions. But the truth was revealed soon enough. On 9 November, the government announced that a new 'revenge weapon' was being used against the capital. Over a thousand of them would make impact by the time the war ended six months later.

On 4 January 1945, one of the rockets landed less than a mile from Pat's house, killing 20 people and leaving a crater around 8m deep. But that death count, as it turned out, was relatively low. Twelve weeks later, when a V-2 hit a block of flats three miles away in Stepney, it left 134 people dead and another 49 seriously injured. And then there was the V-2 strike on a crowded cinema in Antwerp, Belgium, which killed almost 600 people.

Like the V-1s, the V-2s murdered indiscriminately. One of the last to fall, on the morning of 17 March 1945, took the life of a thirteen-year-old girl called Audrey Dear who lived in Woolwich, the other side of the river from Pat's home in West Ham. Audrey's body could only be identified thanks to the ring on one of her fingers, and all that was left of her beloved pet dog was a collection of bones.

All told, the so-called 'flying bomb war' took the lives of almost 9,000 Londoners, a fraction of the tens of thousands who had perished in the Blitz four years earlier. The vengeance weapons were a terrifying menace, but ultimately London was uncowed.

On 27 March 1945, the last V-2 rocket fell to earth in Orpington, Kent, leading to just one fatality. The final doodlebug crash-landed harmlessly two days later.

By now, the writing was on the wall for the Germans.

Allied forces had crossed the Rhine and were rapidly closing in on Berlin.

Less than six weeks later, on 7 May 1945, Pat and the rest of her extended family were on their way home from the pub. The usual gathering was livelier than ever since her uncles Stanley and Tom were both back in London on leave.

When a rumour started going around that the German forces had surrendered unconditionally, Pat's uncles were overwhelmed with emotion. They threw themselves down on the ground with a great cheer, rolling around in the rubble of the nearest bombsite like pigs in muck, and covering their uniforms in dust.

Pat's family had always known how to party, but she had never seen them celebrate quite like this before.

16

VICTORY IN EUROPE

Three miles away in Old Ford Road, Bow, Maureen Hunt and her family heard the news of Germany's surrender on the radio.

By now her brother and sister had long-since returned from their wartime sojourn in the countryside, and the whole family was together in the kitchen, enjoying the light music offered by the BBC.

Then suddenly, at 7.40 p.m., there came a surprise message. 'We are interrupting programmes to make the following announcement,' declared the BBC's veteran newsreader John Snagge.

Everyone in the Hunt family stopped what they were doing, their eyes turning towards the radio. Instinctively, Maureen's mother stood up from her chair.

'It is understood,' Snagge continued, 'that, in accordance with arrangements between the three great powers, an official announcement will be broadcast by the prime minister at three o'clock tomorrow, Tuesday afternoon, the eighth of May. In view of this fact, tomorrow, Tuesday, will be treated as Victory in Europe Day, and will be regarded as a holiday.'

Bizarrely, the announcement never actually mentioned the German surrender, but it was clear to everyone listening – even nine-year-old Maureen – what 'Victory in Europe Day' implied.

Earlier that day, the BBC had mentioned 'unconfirmed reports from correspondents' that indicated an unconditional surrender had been signed in the early hours of the morning.

Then, Maureen's mother had dismissed it as mere rumour. After six years of war, nobody wanted to have their hopes raised only to be dashed again. Now, though, her response was less restrained. All of a sudden, she burst out laughing.

One by one, Maureen, her siblings and even their dad joined in, until the whole family was giggling hysterically at the almost unfathomable news. Then the laughter gave way to tears as the full import of the announcement sank in.

Six years of repressed emotions exploded in a cacophony of laughing and sobbing. It was some minutes before the Hunts managed to get a hold of themselves and were able to speak again.

'Thank God!' exclaimed Mrs Hunt, closing her eyes and crossing herself devoutly.

By now, their neighbours on Old Ford Road were already responding to the news. Every door on the street had been thrown open and radios were blasting at top volume for the benefit of anyone who hadn't heard it yet.

Soon, stunned silence had given way to wild jubila-tion. As the Hunts emerged on to the street, they were embraced by friends and strangers alike, all of them in the grip of the same confused emotions they were feeling.

But before long, any trace of sadness or melancholy had given way to untrammelled joy, and the street party to end all street parties was in full swing. The Hunts' neigh-bour Joey Jones wheeled his piano out into the road and began a lively rendition of 'Roll Out the Barrel'.

Sure enough, before the song had finished, a couple of the neighbourhood's menfolk had already returned home from the local pub bearing barrels of beer, which they had been rolling down the road as fast as they could. Victory in Europe Day might not be starting for another twelve hours but Old Ford Street was in no mood to wait.

It was the start of an epic three-night celebration, the like of which Maureen and her siblings had never seen. There were chairs provided courtesy of the local church hall and party hats made out of old newspaper. The years of wartime rationing were suddenly forgotten as the kids tucked into a platter of shrimp sandwiches and Smiths crisps, washed down with lemonade and cream soda. Then for afters there was a combination of jelly and blancmange. Despite living in one of the poorest parts of London, Maureen suddenly felt like a millionaire.

And through it all, Joey kept the whole neighbourhood entertained with a never-ending repertoire of songs on the piano. He couldn't read a note of music but was more than capable of playing whatever they requested – everything from the latest American songs to Cockney classics like 'Knees Up Mother Brown', 'The Lambeth Walk' and 'Knocked 'Em in the Old Kent Road'.

At nine years old, Maureen had never experienced anything like it in her life.

Meanwhile, up and down the country, other Blitz Kids were enjoying their own local celebrations. A hundred miles away in Birmingham, ten-year-old Dorothy Kedwards had been helping her dad prepare for the big night for weeks. Ever since Allied forces reached Berlin, it had become clear that Victory in Europe was a matter of when, not if – and Dorothy's neighbours, as ever, were well prepared.

Her dad had been voted the neighbourhood's unofficial treasurer, responsible for gathering sixpence a week from all the local people and safely storing the cash in a sock drawer at home. Dorothy's job was to follow him around with a little notebook and keep track of who had contributed. Other families, meanwhile, would be in charge of pooling the local area's ration coupons and purchasing the food and drink.

Mrs Kedwards, though, was more concerned with what Dorothy would be wearing. When the big day came, all the kids were dressed up to the nines, with outfits in red, white and blue. Dorothy's mum was determined to get her hands on some coloured ribbons and searched every shop in the district until eventually she found them. Then she carefully plaited her daughter's hair with the colours of the Union Jack.

In Spitalfields, Kitty Simmonds was enjoying a quiet celebration with her family. Her father had returned from his wartime work building huts for the army and was back with his wife and brother-in-law Yudi. Unlike her uncle, Kitty's parents were not really drinkers, but for VE Day Mr Simmonds was willing to make an exception. 'Come on, let's have a drink,' he told his wife cheerfully, pouring out a bottle of beer.

Kitty, meanwhile, announced she was going 'up west' with two of her girlfriends, Esther Levy and Hetty Schaffer. They soon picked up a couple of boys from the local youth club, and the group began traipsing through the city together, past St Paul's and up to the start of the Strand. Here the lads found a wheelbarrow discarded by the side of the road and insisted the girls climb on board. 'Get in the barrow and we'll push you to Piccadilly!' suggested a boy called Davie Marks.

Kitty and her friends did as they were told, bumping along the pavement all the way along the Strand and up Haymarket to Piccadilly Circus. The famous statue of Eros had been removed thanks to the German bombing campaign, but an American GI stood in its place, locked in a clinch with his British girlfriend. All around, American servicemen were snogging local girls.

'Let's go to Buckingham Palace,' suggested Hetty, and the little group made their way up The Mall, pushing past the crowds until they were close enough to see the famous balcony. Some young people had taken things a step further, shimmying up lampposts to get the best possible view.

Eventually, a group of tiny figures appeared on the balcony: the king, queen and the two princesses, Elizabeth and Margaret. The future queen was dressed smartly in her ATS uniform.

Thousands of spectators erupted in cheers, waving little Union Jack flags.

Before long, the royal family were joined by an even more popular figure: Winston Churchill. For once, the grouchy-looking prime minister was beaming from ear to ear.

It was after midnight by the time Kitty and her friends made it home, walking arm in arm through the streets of London. But in Spitalfields, the party was still in full force, fuelled by beer from the local Truman's Brewery.

Uncle Yudi, in particular, was having the time of his life, singing some of the rudest music-hall songs that Kitty had ever heard and planting kisses on all the prettiest local girls.

Sadly, some of the Blitz Kids missed out on all the VE Day fun. Audrey Hodges, in Bristol, was working the night shift at Frenchay House, now a young adult and responsible for her own cohort of little children. Meanwhile, up in Birmingham, six-year-old Brian Ingram was stuck in bed with a nasty case of chickenpox. Watching the bonfire in the street outside through his window, poor Brian spent the whole evening in floods of tears. When his older brother Malcolm popped his head round the door to show off some fireworks he'd got hold of for the occasion, and tell him all about the incredible food on offer down below, it did little to improve his mood.

For most children, however, VE Day was a feast like no other. In Liverpool, Frances Twigg scoffed cake, jelly and trifle, while in Belfast, Doreen McBride munched on iced buns at a street party that soon turned into a literal bun-fight.

As the nation adjusted to peacetime, new foods began to appear in the shops as well. Maureen Hunt was amazed to receive her first ever banana, and immediately bit down on the thick, rubbery skin. 'No, no!' her mother exclaimed, laughing. 'You have to peel it first!' Other kids were equally baffled by the sight of fresh oranges. Some younger children began playing catch with them, not realising that the little brightly coloured balls were edible.

Fruit wasn't the only puzzling new arrival. As fathers who had been serving in the forces began to arrive home, a generation of young children had to adjust to sharing a house with men who in some cases were little more than strangers. One seven-year-old boy's father, desperate to bond with him again, insisted on them taking baths together, despite his son's discomfort.

Some fathers returned very different from how their children remembered them. One little girl in West London barely recognised her dad, who had lost several stone and returned in an emaciated state after spending time in a prisoner-of-war camp. He later took his own life, following an army reunion that brought back painful memories.

As the war in Europe came to an end, children were reckoning with challenging new concepts. Ever since the liberation of Bergen-Belsen in April 1945, British civilians had begun to get an understanding of the terrible inhumanity of the Holocaust. One Jewish schoolboy in Manchester was horrified by footage from the concentration camp, which he saw in a Pathé newsreel screened before a movie he'd gone to see with his parents.

Then there was the bombing of the Japanese cities of Hiroshima and Nagasaki, which took place three months after VE Day and brought the war in the Far East to an end. The spectre of the atomic terror, which would dominate the lives of Blitz Kids all over the world in the decades that followed, wasn't always understood right away. One young boy misread a newspaper headline and thought that two 'COMIC BOMBS' had been dropped in Japan, unable to imagine what this cartoonish new threat might be.

Gradually, the privations and horrors of wartime gave way to a more optimistic landscape. Food was still rationed, and much of the bomb damage of the war years remained – a boon to any Blitz Kids still young enough to enjoy the pleasures of playing on the bombsites. But in other respects, life was gradually returning to normal. An education system that had been coming apart at the seams was given a radical overhaul thanks to the implementation of the 1944 Education Act, which brought in free second-ary education for all.

The world of entertainment, too, was growing, as cinemas and theatres expanded their previously limited repertoires. Although most had remained open during the war years, many parents had been understandably wary of letting their kids disappear into dark, often poorly protected buildings. Now there was plenty of catching up to do.

Maureen Hunt and her father had already seen *The Wizard of Oz* half a dozen times when the movie's star, Judy Garland, arrived in London to sing at the Palladium. Mr Hunt, who had always been a fan of musicals, bought tickets for the whole family to see her.

Maureen gaped open-mouthed as Judy belted out her trademark song 'Over the Rainbow', dressed in a beautiful gown. The magical world she described, where troubles melt like lemon drops, had never felt so real before.

The lemon drops themselves might have to wait, though. With sweets still on the ration until 1953, it would be a while before the Blitz Kids could fully indulge their sweet tooths.

Epilogue

Eventually, even the youngest of the Blitz Kids were kids no longer. Their generation, whose formative years had been spent amid the rubble of wartime, grew up and set off on their own adventures, just as every other generation had before them. But they took with them something of the unique experience they had lived through as children.

MAUREEN HUNT met her husband, Joe Donovan, at her twenty-first birthday party. He was eighteen years older than her and had gone through the war as an adult. Joe gave her a very different perspective on the war to the one she'd had as a child, telling her about his harrowing experience of opening the gas chambers at Auschwitz to find human bodies rolling out of them. 'I've seen man's inhumanity to man,' he told her sadly.

It was an experience that never fully left Joe, a quiet man with the calmest temperament of anyone Maureen knew. 'When you've seen what I have, you don't lose your temper over silly little things,' he explained.

For her own part, Maureen feels that living through the Blitz made her more resilient. In 2001, after caring for Joe for four years, she lost him to Parkinson's, and then lost both her daughters to cancer.

'People say to me, "I don't know how you keep standing," and I say, "I think my strength from the war helps me,"' she told us. 'The grandchildren are growing up and my son-in-law needs support. What good would it do if I just sat here crying, when people need me?'

Kitty Simmonds, who had fought so hard to stay in the East End during the war, ultimately ended up leaving it for a new life thousands of miles away. She met Canadian Ralph Wintrob at a Passover celebration when he was visiting Britain with his mother. At thirty-two years old, Kitty married Ralph and crossed the Atlantic with him to start a new life in Toronto. Ralph got a job as a school librarian, and they had two children together, Suzanne and Phillip. After Kitty's father passed away, her mother came to join her in Canada, but sadly died eighteen months later of cancer.

When she became a mum herself, Kitty finally understood her mother's deep fears for her safety during the Blitz, and felt sorry for having caused her so much worry. Tragically, the very loss Mrs Simmonds had been so worried about later came true for Kitty herself, when her own son, Phillip, died at the age of seventeen in a car accident.

Like many Blitz Kids, Kitty felt a strong duty to pass on the story of what happened to her during the war to future generations. Despite losing her eyesight in her mid-seventies, she wrote a memoir of her experiences as an evacuee, spending the next few years touring schools, libraries and book clubs with the help of her husband, Ralph. After sending the queen a copy of her book, she was even invited to attend a garden party at Buckingham Palace in May 2020, but sadly was unable to go because of the Covid-19 pandemic. At ninety-eight, Kitty doesn't get out as much as she used to, but she still enjoys giving online talks on Zoom.

Robert Wickens still lives in the East End, just up the road from the house his family moved to towards the end of the war. After doing his National Service at the age of eighteen, he became a bus conductor. A friend who worked on the buses with him set him up on a blind date with his sister, and Robert ended up marrying her.

When he wanted to take his wife on holiday, Robert had to apply for a passport for the first time. Unsure what to put in the box on the form that asked for his father's name, he simply didn't fill it in.

'Excuse me, sir, you've left this blank,' the clerk at the passport office pointed out to him. 'Are you illegitimate?'

In front of a queue of a dozen fellow customers, Robert was forced to acknowledge the truth out loud for the first time. 'Yeah,' he replied. 'I think I am.'

He was aware of the other people staring at him, finally coming face to face with the shame that had dogged his family for so many years, forcing them to move house again and again throughout his childhood.

But Robert didn't feel ashamed. As far as he was

concerned, neither he nor his mother, Mary, had done anything wrong. 'You can't alter it,' he told us philosophically. 'It's never really worried me.'

BRIAN INGRAM now lives on the outskirts of Birmingham, four miles away from the house where he grew up in Balsall Heath. After the war, he left school and did his National Service, before getting a job as a motor mechanic. He developed a passion for cycling, riding around the Isle of Wight, Cornwall, Scotland and the South of France.

Brian got married in 1965. He and his wife never had children, but they lived happily together until 1996, when she got sick and Brian was forced to take early retirement. For the next eight years he cared for her, until she died in 2004.

He's still in touch with his elder brother, Malcolm, but relations haven't always been easy – and the legacy of the war years still hangs over them. 'To this day, we don't really get on, and I think it's because he was evacuated,' Brian told us. 'I think he felt not wanted.'

'Even now it's brought up, that I wasn't evacuated and he was. And I'm eighty-six and he's ninety!'

DOROTHY KEDWARDS's artistic talent won her a place at Bourneville Art School, after her teacher applied on her behalf without telling her. But she decided to turn it down. 'I loved art, but I didn't want it to be my whole life,' she explained. 'I was a free spirit and there were so many things I wanted to do.'

Instead, when she left school at fifteen, Dorothy took a job at the BSA factory in Birmingham, working as secretary to the personnel manager. The legacy of the horrific bombing the factory had endured during the Blitz still haunted workers there, many of whom were convinced that there were unrecovered bodies lying under the ruined New Building. But for Dorothy the BSA was a fresh start and a place of fun and friendship. After the war ended, the factory's output had reverted from guns to motorbikes, and since Dorothy's job took her all over the factory site, she got to know the lads who tested the latest models. When no one was looking, they'd let her jump on the back and go for a spin with them.

Dorothy later went to work at Morris Motors, where she met her husband, an engineer. They were married within twelve months and went to live on the Yorkshire Moors, where they spent many happy years before returning to the Midlands, settling in the quiet Worcestershire village of Dodford.

After Dorothy's husband died in the late 1990s of a brain tumour, she kept herself busy running an antiques shop with her sister Angela and nephew Ian, later moving to Droitwich Spa to be closer to them. But she never abandoned her artistic side, devoting much of her free time, arthritis allowing, to various projects: watercolours, pencil sketches and intricate Victorian dioramas, depicting street scenes and house interiors in immaculate detail – very like the doll's house she once made as a lonely evacuee in Worcester during the war.

DOREEN JOHNSON still lives in Coventry, although the city has changed immeasurably during her lifetime. She met her husband, Tommy, at a local youth club, and married him in 1955. To her disappointment, they never had children, but Doreen, a woman of strong religious faith, took it as an opportunity. 'I decided our Lord meant for me to do something else,' she told us.

Inspired by the example she had seen in the Blitz on Coventry, of ordinary people helping each other through the toughest of times, Doreen devoted her life to charity work. Through her church, she was able to help kids in a village in Africa, and when the canoes they relied on were stolen, she paid to replace them herself. The photo she later received showing the children with their new canoes is one of her most treasured possessions.

After a lifetime of helping others, four years ago at the age of eighty-six Doreen decided she needed a bit of help herself and moved into a nursing home. She now spends much of her free time attending Zoom meetings with the management committee and coordinating the team of young men who tend the gardens.

'I know it's called a rest home, but I like to keep busy,' she laughs. 'The way I see it, our Lord must like the flowers, so he's decided to leave me here a bit longer.'

BETTY ALLEN trained as a cook after leaving school and fell in love with a sailor called Ron at the age of eighteen. They got married and moved to Bath, where she still lives today.

Thanks to the example of devotion set by her own parents, Betty and her husband had a very happy marriage. She claims they never argued once in all of their sixty-four years together, and to meet Betty today you can well believe it.

As a little girl, Betty had lost her beloved twin dolls when her house in Filton was obliterated by a German bomb, but in later years they inspired her to take up a new hobby. She now makes her own dolls, with beautiful porcelain faces, which she sells on eBay.

These days, Betty is housebound, but her three devoted children take care of her, visiting or FaceTiming with her every day. While living alone, she has learned to ask Amazon's Alexa what's going on in the world outside.

After she got married, AUDREY HODGES carried on working as a nursery teacher for the kids at Downend. Once she and her husband had their own flat, she began bringing one child home with her every weekend. Audrey loved her work with the orphans, but eventually she had to leave as she found it too upsetting seeing the state they were in some mornings: turning up without shoes, with unbrushed hair and the remains of breakfast still on their faces. She and her husband ended up taking over her dad's shop, just as he had wanted, and then opening another of their own.

After moving on from Downend and becoming a mother herself, Audrey thought she'd put the children there behind her. But later in life she became involved with a project to track down the American GIs and reunite them with their grown-up children.

Now aged ninety-seven, she still lives independently in the house she and her husband moved into sixty years ago.

Despite her father's undermining words, DOREEN HENRY went on to become the first woman in her family to go to university, following her life-long passion for animals by studying zoology. Later, she became a teacher. She always made a point of encouraging her pupils and treating them with respect, just like her beloved Mrs Armstrong had done all those years ago.

Doreen was determined not to give up her career once she had children. She blazed a trail in the 1960s by becoming the first woman at her school to return to work after giving birth, going back after the paltry six weeks' maternity leave. 'I felt I hadn't spent years studying for a degree to sit at home scratching!' she told us. Doreen was expecting the headmaster to say she couldn't do her job any more, but luckily he was a forward-thinking man and allowed her to go part-time for the first term.

When the Troubles began, she and her family moved to Lisburn, eight miles outside Belfast. Their new house was under a flight path and Doreen suddenly found herself waking up sweating with fear in the night, as the sound of the planes overhead brought back memories of the Blitz. It took her a year to be able to sleep through the night.

Later, Doreen faced up to her difficult memories when

she wrote a book about her own and other children's wartime experiences in Northern Ireland.

As a child Doreen had struggled to cope with her dad's volatile moods, but as an adult she came to see that they were caused by manic depression. She did her best to take care of her father after her mother died, making his meals five nights a week, but in his old age he became increasingly abusive. Eventually she was forced to make the difficult decision to cut him out of her life altogether.

After the war, sweeping changes took place in Liverpool, and many of the old tenement blocks were knocked down. FRANCES TWIGG's large family were moved out of their flat and into a brand-new, four-bedroom council house with hot and cold water, electricity and an indoor bathroom. But progress came at a cost, as the old communities were broken up and dispersed.

Frances went on to work at the Tate & Lyle factory that she had lived opposite as a child. She grew up to be just as beautiful as her mother and in 1951 won the company's beauty contest. She returned to the factory after having her children and was chosen to be its official tour guide, showing lord mayors and politicians around the refinery.

Over a year ago, at the age of ninety, Frances had a fall while making a cup of tea and broke her hip. She's still waiting for a new one, and in the meantime is more or less bedbound.

Despite her months of missed education thanks to the Liverpool Blitz, CLARA GREEN became the first person in her family to win a scholarship to grammar school. Her parents got a grant to cover the cost of the school coat but buying the rest of the uniform was a struggle for them. Clara felt conspicuously different from the other girls there, who made it clear she didn't fit in, and she ended up leaving.

Clara went to work at the Littlewood Pools, and at twenty married a man eleven years older than her called Joe McGann. Joe had been a navy commando in the war and was one of the first men to make it ashore on D-Day, but he had been invalided out after a German grenade exploded near him. Although he recovered from his physical injuries, his wartime trauma had left him with a diagnosis of 'anxiety neurosis' – now known as PTSD – causing him to be moody and depressive at times. When Clara found out about the diagnosis and tried to speak to him about it, he was furious and refused to discuss it. Nor would he talk to his wife about the baby twins they lost at twenty-six weeks, in the misguided belief, shared by so many men of his generation, that speaking about their pain would only make it worse.

Clara went on to have five more children. While they were still young, she went back to education and eventually qualified as a teacher. Her children say the example she set helped inspire them to follow their own dreams – all four of the McGann boys went on to become successful actors.

CHRISTOPHER MUNRO had left borstal determined to turn his life around, and for a while he settled down, working steady jobs, getting married and having three kids. But a few years later he was tempted back into a life of crime, stealing copper wire from a warehouse. He got caught, aged thirty, when the police stopped him because his getaway lorry had a broken headlight.

Christopher was sent to Strangeways Prison in Manchester to serve a six-month sentence. It was a terrible experience, and being unable to hug his kids when they came to visit him was heartbreaking. Christopher went back to his cell and wept, feeling ashamed and miserable. He vowed that when he got out, he would never turn to crime again.

When he left prison in September 1969, he borrowed £50 from his mother-in-law and set himself up as a cab driver. Soon he was running a whole fleet of cars as well as a garage. He went on to own an empire that included properties, a nightclub, betting shops and a bed and breakfast, eventually becoming a millionaire. The entrepreneurial spirit he had forged during the war had served him well.

After his wife, Esther, died of breast cancer, Christopher began fundraising for cancer charities, going on to raise thousands of pounds. 'I think it's clear I've done some bad things,' he told us, 'but I feel the good I've done in the world outweighs the bad.'

During the pandemic, Chrisopher contracted Covid and was in intensive care for five months. When he survived, the doctors nicknamed him 'the miracle man'. Despite still having long Covid, at eighty-six he is physically fit and active and goes dancing several times a week.

After going back to Guernsey, JOHN LE PAGE met a girl called Joan, who had just returned from spending the war in Scotland with her mother. Joan's father had remained on the island throughout the war and was horrified to hear his daughter attempting to speak the old Guernsey patois in her new Glaswegian accent.

As a fellow evacuee, John felt an instant connection to Joan, and he began attending her church every Sunday just so he could see her. They always sat together in the back row, holding hands and trading stories of the war years in Britain.

A few years later, the couple got married and decided to move into John's grandmother's old house, a small cottage by the sea. It was very run-down, with no gas, no electricity, no running water and a toilet at the bottom of the garden. But thanks to the DIY skills he had picked up at school in Bath, John was able to turn it into a dream home for the two of them.

With the help of Joan's dad, a professional builder, he gutted the old kitchen, built a new single-storey extension and put in a new bathroom and toilet. After losing his own father in the war, John enjoyed working with his father-in-law.

Seven decades later, John and Joan are still living in the cottage, where they raised their children. Beyond the bottom of their garden, past John's greenhouse overflowing with strawberries and tomatoes, the Channel stretches into the distance: a hundred miles of sea, leading all the way to England.

And in a cupboard under the stairs sits his dad's old red suitcase, with the German tail fin tucked inside it.

At the age of eighty-six, IRENE BROWN still lives in Southampton. During her many decades in the port city, she and her husband, Dennis, ran three pubs there together. One of them, the Royal Standard, looks out over the Western Esplanade, where Irene watched the American soldiers departing on D-Day.

Today, the imposing building has reinvented itself as a boutique hotel, though some locals remain convinced that the ghost of a nineteenth-century prostitute who hanged herself in the scullery still haunts its corridors. Meanwhile, the fourteenth-century Undercroft on Upper Bugle Street, where Irene and her family sheltered during the war, now serves as a trendy music venue.

Irene and Dennis raised three sons together, Barry, Mark and Pete. Sadly, Dennis died in 2011 at the age of seventy-seven, and Pete passed away unexpectedly just last year.

When she left school, PAT PEACHAM dreamed of becoming a dress designer but her father refused to pay for her training. She took a job as a machinist in a clothing factory, before working at John Knight's soap factory and Tate & Lyle's sugar refinery in Silvertown, East London.

Pat loved going out with her friends, dancing, roller-skating and going to the pictures. After a while she got fed up of working shifts at the refinery, since they interfered with her social life, so she got a job working on the railways instead.

When she was seventeen, she met Tony, a painter and decorator, and married him two years later. It was a happy marriage and they had two sons together, but looking back Pat thinks she might have done things differently. 'You were brought up to think that was your aim – to get married and have children,' she told us. 'As much as I loved my husband, if I had my life again I'd like to travel and work abroad like my granddaughters.'

The couple later moved to Clacton-on-Sea. When Pat retired, she finally got a chance to explore her artistic side and still goes to an art club every week, painting by the sea. Life hasn't always been a bed of roses, but she tries to have a positive attitude.

'I make the best of everything, whatever the situation,' she said. 'I've had cancer, but my attitude is there's nothing you can do about it, so you just have to enjoy what you can.'

Pat and her cousin Terry have never forgotten the day they narrowly missed being killed by a doodlebug and witnessed bodies being pulled out of the rubble. 'I can still see it, plain as anything,' Pat told us. 'You never forget something like that.'

For Terry, the trauma resurfaced a few years later, when he was doing his National Service in Cyprus. After a petrol bomb went off near him, he developed severe alopecia, losing all the hair on his head and elsewhere on his body. An air force doctor told him the incident had probably triggered his unconscious trauma from the earlier bombing. Terry's hair never grew back and for years he wore a wig, but after shaved heads became more fashionable he stopped bothering with it.

Terry is far from the only Blitz Kid we spoke to whose trauma from the war years resurfaced unexpectedly in later life. In Coventry, Doreen Johnson was taking the lift in a department store when it broke down and she found herself trapped for fifteen minutes. Suddenly she began having a panic attack, hyperventilating and feeling faint, as the experience brought back the claustrophobia she had felt in her grandmother's Anderson shelter.

In 1995, Brian Ingram attended a museum exhibition marking fifty years since the end of the war. He had never previously shown any signs of post-traumatic stress, but the re-creation of a wartime air-raid siren caught him completely off guard. Brian fled from the museum and never went back.

Yet Brian claimed he had never felt afraid as a child during the air raids. 'I wasn't scared,' he told us. 'Mum was probably terrified, but I was too young.'

Researching this book, we were surprised how many of our interviewees said the same thing. 'To us children, it didn't affect us like it did the older people,' Frances Twigg told us. 'They were worried, but it was all a story to us.'

Psychological research conducted by Anna Freud and others during the war years appears to bear this out. 'So long as bombing incidents occur when small children are in the care of their mothers or a familiar mother substitute, they do not seem particularly affected by them,' Freud observed. 'Their experience remains an "accident".'

In fact, Freud's surprising discovery was that separation from their mothers was actually more traumatic for many children than enduring bombing raids, suggesting that the evacuation campaign in the early months of the war was deeply misguided. As psychoanalyst Edward Glover put it in 1942, 'All the advantages in safety, health or comfort to be gained under evacuation conditions may dwindle to nothing when weighed against the fact that the child has to lose his family in order to gain them.'

Among Blitz Kids who stayed behind and witnessed the bombing first-hand, even those who told us they found it frightening generally claim it left no lasting effect on them. We lost count of the number of interviewees who told us, 'We just got on with it,' when we tried to ask them about the impact of their experiences.

At a time when mental health was poorly understood, and there were no counsellors available to offer therapy to traumatised children, they had little other choice. Having had to cope as best they could, their generation can often be resentful at what they see as the mollycoddling of today's children and the growing numbers of youngsters being diagnosed with anxiety or depression.

Many believe their Blitz experiences made them stronger, instilling a grit and determination that have seen them through the rest of their lives. One of our interviewees told us that she and her friends have a mantra that has helped them deal with divorce, illness, bereavement and more: 'We survived the Blitz. We can survive anything.'

As they approach the final stage of their lives, our Blitz Kids look back on the war with a mixture of sadness and pride. For many, it was a time of deprivation and hardship, of loss, worry and fear. But in amongst such difficult memories are happier thoughts as well – of the strong bonds of family and community that helped them make it through, and the kindness of strangers at the darkest of moments.

They're aware too that while growing up in wartime is an alien experience to most British people, around the world not all children are so lucky. Watching news reports from contemporary war zones, former Blitz Kids see their own experiences reflected in the lives of war's youngest victims.

'It makes me feel ill, seeing the bombs in Gaza and Ukraine,' Doreen Henry told us. 'Because I remember being under the stairs with my mother and being absolutely terrified.'

Acknowledgements

Our thanks are due first and foremost to the amazing men and women whose stories fill the pages of this book: Maureen Donovan (née Hunt), Kitty Wintrob (née Simmonds), Robert Wickens, Brian Ingram, Dorothy Humphries (née Kedwards), Doreen Cadden (née Johnson), Betty Peachey (née Allen), Audrey Spearing (née Hodges), Doreen McBride (née Henry), Frances Izzard (née Twigg), Clara McGann (née Green), Chris Munro, John Le Page, Irene Christian (née Brown), Pat Johnston (née Peacham) and Terry Marshall. Thanks also to their families, friends and carers, who helped make our interviews with them possible – in particular Anthony Edwards, Suzanne Wintrob, Ralph Wintrob, Nadine Webster, Stephen McGann, Mark McGann, Chrysta Roberts and Barry Christian.

Some of our Blitz Kids have written their own accounts of their wartime experiences. Kitty Wintrob's memoir, *I'm Not Going Back*, is an engaging and evocative account of her evacuation experience, Chris Munro's *Seen It All, Done It All* offers a no-holds-barred account of growing up in the slums of Liverpool, while Doreen McBride's *We Just Got On With It* gathers together the fascinating accounts of dozens of men and women who lived through the war in Northern Ireland.

During our research, we spoke to many more than just the fifteen people who feature in this book, and we are grateful to all our interviewees for taking the time to share their memories with us. You can read more of their stories at www.blitzkids.co.uk. If you or anyone you know remembers the war, we would love to hear from you.

For their generous help finding interviewees and setting up meetings, thanks to Geoff Gardiner at the Whitchurch Local History Society, Garry Atterton at the Barton Hill History Group, John Freeland at the Stratford Society, Margot Galvin, Francesca Whiting, Alex Derber, Sally Williams, Barbara Beebe Jensen, Steve and Peta Benson, and our wonderful agent, Laura MacDougall. Thanks also to Julia Indelicate for help with transcribing our interviews.

It was our longtime editor Iain MacGregor who originally commissioned this book, and Martin Redfern and Ellie Harris at Headline have expertly shepherded it through writing and production. Emma Horton sensitively copy-edited the manuscript and Darren Rugg offered helpful comments on an early draft.

And thanks, of course, to Henry Southgate – whose little piece of shrapnel first inspired us to write to write about Blitz Kids like him.